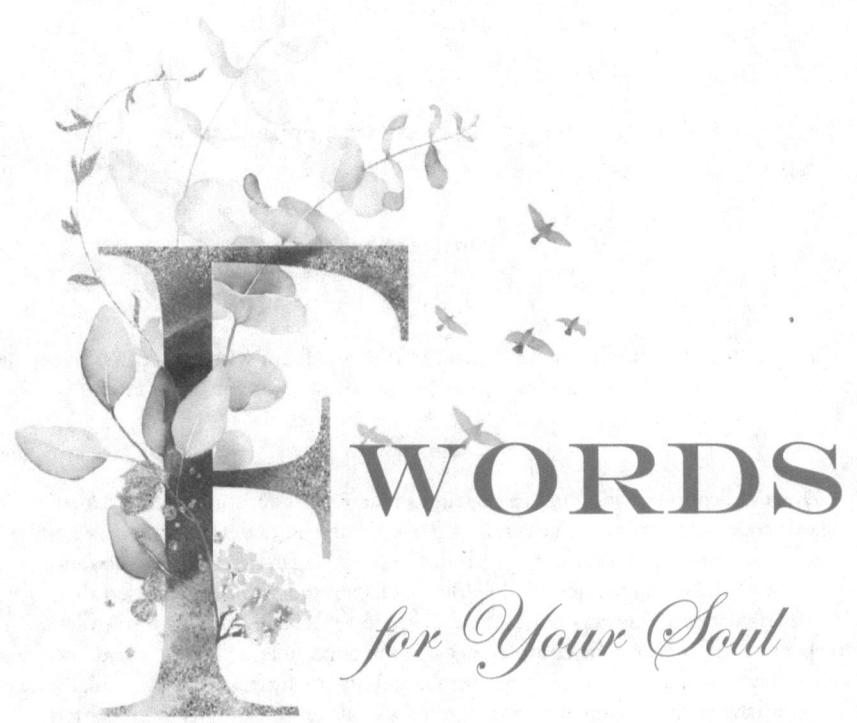

F WORDS

for Your Soul

KIM LITTRELL

Book Cover by Klassic Designs

1st edition 2024

ISBN: 979-8-9919118-0-1

DEDICATION

To Knox Ryan & Khloe Rose:
This book would not be without you.
May it inspire you to create a life
beyond your wildest dreams.

CONTENTS

ACKNOWLEDGMENTS

I'd like to thank my husband, first and foremost, for supporting my dreams and giving me the time and space to write this book, for allowing me to put the intimate details of our lives out there for the world to see, and for always being my rock and constant reminder to look on the bright side.

There were many people along the way whose kind words gave me the push that I needed to keep trudging forward along this journey. To each of you, I will be forever grateful. Thank you for giving me the confidence to pursue my dreams.

To my best friend, Daisha Lile, thank you for being an early reader of my work when I was too embarrassed to even tell anyone that I was writing a book! Your encouragement and words of affirmation were the first glimpse I had into the idea that maybe, *just maybe*, I really could write something great.

Thank you to Cara Lockwood, an early developmental editor, who sang my praises when I barely even had a fully formed concept. It was you who told me that this was not a children's book, saving me countless hours trying to make it one! It was an easy choice to ask you to complete the final edit before print as well.

Thank you to Tavia Cathcart Brown for finding me that day, for telling me exactly what I needed to hear, and for being so giving of your time and encouragement. You were perhaps the only reason I kept going at a time when I was so ready to give up. I am certain that you are an angel.

Thank you to Ty Gideon Love for your edit of my first complete, yet *very* rough draft, for helping me with the dreaded book proposal, and for offering all of your publishing knowledge to me so freely. Your acknowledgement of me as a talented writer when you had worked with so many acclaimed authors meant more to me than you could ever know. Your question, *is this how you want to tell your children this story?* echoed through my ears throughout many rewrites. It is, I believe, what made this book all that it is – something that I can be incredibly proud of.

Thank you to my parents for being so supportive and encouraging. Always wanting to make you proud, it was the two of you whom I was most afraid to hand my book over to. It was one of the best moments of my life when you told me how deeply it affected you and made you see the world in a different way. It was then that I knew I was ready to see this journey all the way through to the end.

PREFACE

Dear Reader,

It is my hope that the title of this book has drawn you to it — that you have picked it up on your own accord. That the size of it is not intimidating, but welcoming. That it is laid out in such a manner that you can not only consume it all at once, but also easily reference individual pieces for years to come.

I do not intend for this book to act so much as a bible to you, an end-all, be-all, of blind faith in someone else's words, no more than I would want the bible itself to act as such in your life. Rather, this is meant to provide you with a foundation strong enough that you can build upon it your own truths for years to come. It is the knowledge I have gained along the way that I wish I could go back and tell *myself* when I was younger.

I have lived an extraordinary life, one in which many of my dreams have come true. I wouldn't change a thing as everything I have experienced has brought me to this exact moment in time, here with you, experiencing a happiness beyond my wildest dreams. But I do sometimes wonder, if I'd known this magic sooner, how interesting life would have been — the confidence I would have felt, the chances I may have taken, the adventures I may have embarked upon.

That is my hope for you, that this book enables you to embark upon *your own* grand adventures. That you have the courage, time and time again, to leap even when the net has yet to appear. That you not waste a single moment of

1

your life in fear or in doubt, but rather in hopeful anticipation, embracing the glorious uncertainty around every turn.

It is my intention to ignite the spark that lies deep within you and to stoke the fire as you boldly blaze your own trail that leads toward your deepest desires, rather than blindly following the herd on one of the more "practical" or "safe" paths already laid out for you. I hope your yellow brick road brings you adventure and deeply hidden truths that both startle and awaken you. And I hope that by taking the road less traveled you lead a magical, nonsensical life beyond *your* wildest dreams too.

If nothing else, I hope this book encourages you to embrace your curiosity and childlike sense of wonder within. To return to your three-year-old default state of *why?* And to question everything, *especially* the status quo. To not only ask the right kinds of questions, but to ask the right source. For the quality of the questions you ask *yourself* will determine the quality of your life.

Follow every passion and inspiration as it comes. Study fiercely every subject that interests you. Learn as much as you can about yourself, about others, about this beautiful world that we live in, and that which is beyond it. And then, go within, and find all the answers you will ever need. For *YOU* are your greatest teacher, and once you understand that, you understand *everything*. There is an infinite intelligence and almighty power that resides within you. You need only learn how to tap into it.

Once you understand how to cultivate and wield this power intentionally, the world around you will become your playground. And just like the playdoh you loved as a child, reality will become yours to play with, to mold and to shape into anything your imagination can create.

Anything you desire is possible.

I repeat: *Anything* is possible. And it is *all* within *you*.

> *"Above all, watch with glittering eyes the whole world*
> *around you, because the greatest secrets are always*
> *hidden in the most unlikely places. Those who don't*
> *believe in magic will never find it."*
>
> ROALD DAHL

PROLOGUE

"As crazy as it sounds, I truly believe I'll be a millionaire one day."

I'm sure there was a very big eye roll on the other end of the phone. My best friend certainly thought I was crazy most of the time. Luckily, I was her particular kind of crazy (the kind that thoroughly amused her), so I could get away with saying just about anything to her without fear of judgment. This sentence was particularly cringe-worthy though, and it got caught in my throat halfway up as I spit it out. After all, who was I to say such a thing?

It was the year 2019, and at the time, my husband and I were making less than $100k a year, *combined*. We also had no valid reason to believe we'd ever make much more than that. While this thought about becoming a millionaire had been ruminating in my mind for quite some time, I'd never dared say it out loud to anyone before. The only reason it found its way out of my mouth *now* was out of sheer desperation.

My friend had no idea how talented she was. She had a passion and an innate skill that was next level, something I envied about her, but she simply couldn't think any bigger than her nine-to-five job. It was the box that had been carefully selected for her, the box she'd been born into believing was the only one available to her.

My friend's mother was actually an entrepreneur. She never went to college or got a "regular" job. Instead, she owned her own hair salon and was very talented and successful. But it was a hard business – long hours on your feet and no residual income, no paid time off for sickness or vacations, and certainly no benefits. As is so often the case, her mother wanted something different for her child. She wanted her to have options and opportunities that she never had.

Thus, beginning at a young age, it was ingrained within my friend that the best way to live a safe, comfortable life was to go to college and get a job. There was a pressure on her to follow through on this, as she would be the first in her family to do so. As a college graduate, she would make her parents *so* proud.

This was the experience of most of my generation. College, which led to a job with decent pay and good benefits. It was...*just* what you did. It was expected of you. It was how you were supposed to win at life. But it had become increasingly clear to me that this reality was not *really* winning.

I knew my friend was worthy of so much more than the job she was complaining to me about. I wanted to inspire her to think bigger, to think as big as *I* did. Because while I, too, at the time, had a nine-to-five job, I knew that wasn't my final destination. What kept me sane during those forty hours a week, forty-nine weeks a year was knowing that there was a life beyond this that I was striving for, that I was working toward with passion and purpose. It wasn't a life I dreamed of having in thirty to forty years when I retired, but a life that could be obtained *now*. That hope is what kept me thriving every day. I desperately wanted to give my friend that hope as well – to help her imagine a life beyond her wildest dreams, too.

Of course, she couldn't imagine such a thing for herself. Her box was thick and made of steel. Big dreams of becoming a famous stylist or an interior designer were for *other* people – those more talented, more resourced, or just plain luckier than her. No amount of my crazy talk was going to convince her otherwise.

But perhaps this conversation wasn't only about her. Perhaps it was actually *me* who needed the convincing. Maybe finally saying it out loud, this thought about becoming a millionaire, that my mind had been relentlessly chewing on for years, may have been just what *I* needed.

Looking back now, I wonder if at that very moment, by saying the words out loud, "I truly believe I'll be a millionaire one day," it anchored my dream into reality.

Fast forward to 2022.

"I'm only telling you this because you're my best friend, and if I can't tell *you*, then who can I tell?" Once again, I was on the phone with that same friend, talking about being a millionaire, just three years later. Except now, I was doing it from my million-dollar home, with my family on track to net well-over a million dollars that year. And *this* time, there was *no* catch in my throat.

I shared with her that after looking at our finances, I realized that if we just kept doing what we were already doing, we'd have well over a million dollars in assets by the following year.

That's right, we'd be millionaires. It was no longer a dream; it was a *fact*.

So how did we get here? How did my husband and I go from being two kids, raised by middle-class families, to being two adults with barely enough money to scrape by, to… *drum roll, please*…becoming millionaires?

Well, that story starts way back in 2009 in the small town of Richmond, Kentucky.

I met my husband at a bar in our college town and we quickly fell head over heels in love. Kyle had an energy unlike anyone I had ever met, a confidence that was magnetic, and a charisma that drew people to him. He had a knack for finding the humor and fun in all things and spoke positively about every situation. Kyle had *big* dreams and had no doubt that he was made for great things. And even though I often thought he was completely full of it, like a moth to a flame, I couldn't seem to get enough of him.

For a self-proclaimed realist such as myself, his fantastical ideas teetered for me somewhere between a breath of fresh air and complete, and utter, bullshit. He had a new big idea seemingly every week, and he would tell everybody about it as if it were a sure thing, as if the idea were already a reality. Those ideas *rarely* panned out, but it never seemed to faze him. He'd let it roll off his shoulders and would be on to the next big idea before *my* head had a chance to stop spinning.

Nonetheless, when I was around him, I found myself viewing the world through his eyes. It was like wearing rose-colored glasses that showed endless possibilities and potential everywhere. With him, the world around me seemed to come alive with a touch of magic.

Kyle would introduce me to a documentary about quantum physics that would change my life, called *What the Bleep Do We Know? Down the Rabbit Hole*. And down the rabbit hole, I certainly went. I became *obsessed* with quantum physics and the real-life implications of what was possible. It would send me on a journey that I have no doubt changed the trajectory of our entire lives.

It was a short time after I watched that documentary that the book *The Secret* found its way into my orbit and I learned all about the Law of Attraction. These two concepts, the science and the spiritual, came together for me like two pieces of a puzzle that snapped crisply into place to explain the *entire world*. It was a breaking down of everything I *thought* I knew and a rebuilding of a newfound, or perhaps more precisely, *re-found* wisdom. A spirituality, so to speak, supported by science, that I believe I had been searching for my entire life and had always been destined to find.

For the next ten years, I would deep dive into these concepts so feverishly one could call it an obsession. I read, listened to, and watched anything and everything that had to do with quantum physics and the Law of Attraction. My obsession led me down the path of personal development, a topic that is riddled with these concepts. Every single successful person that I read about – from Dale and Andrew Carnegie, John D. Rockefeller and Henry Ford to Steve Jobs, Michael Jordan, Oprah Winfrey, and Jim Carey – *just to name a few* – all seemed to be saying the *exact same thing*. Everything starts with your thoughts and beliefs around what is possible for you. Literally *everything*.

As I studied my husband right alongside these uber-successful people, I began realizing that his extreme confidence and positive thinking was not as insane as I'd once thought it to be. It was actually the *opposite* of this that was insane – people who cut themselves off at the knees, thinking that they didn't have what it took to do whatever they dreamed of doing, people who believed that they *weren't capable* of living extraordinary lives, and didn't think they were *worthy* of abundance and unlimited success and happiness. This was *the epitome* of insanity. Because *why not* you?

The more I learned, the more I experimented, and the more proof I found, the more I knew that reality was far more malleable than I'd been led to believe. And I had far more power than I ever could have imagined. I was indeed creating my own reality, based on my thoughts, beliefs, feelings, and actions. And I was fully in control of my life.

On January 1, 2022, Kyle and I sat down, as we always did, to write out our goals for the upcoming year. Kyle wanted to set a goal of $650k net profit for our family business. A worthy goal, it would almost double what we'd made in 2021. It was well thought out and attainable.

And I said, "Why not a million?" It was our ultimate goal, after all. It was where we'd wanted to eventually arrive. So, why decide to think it would take years to get there? Why not decide to think that we could do it *right now*? He agreed with this logic, and one million dollars went down on the paper.

It was an outlandish goal, one that we had no reason to believe was possible. In fact, it should absolutely *not* have been possible. But, oh, how we have gotten good at creating the impossible. We hit our one-million-dollar goal less than three-quarters of the way through 2022 while the business kept growing, profiting exponentially.

This is how we have made so many of our dreams come true. One of us always pushing the other to remove the box, to identify and discard our limiting beliefs, to raise the ceiling on our upper limits, and to dream bigger, to go higher, to believe in the crazy, the outlandish, the impossible. And perhaps most importantly, to never accept defeat in the pursuit of those dreams.

It did not always appear that we would get here. There were devastating setbacks, failures, and tragedies along the way, and many times we could have given up on our big dreams and settled for the status quo. But even in the face of great adversity, we held on firmly to our belief in what was possible, and created the most beautiful life together, *the life of our dreams*.

This book began as a letter to my son after a phone call on an unexpected morning changed our lives forever. In times such as these, the veil is briefly lifted, and one is reminded just how delicate the fabric of our reality truly is, how easily it can be torn to shreds in just a single moment.

Forced to come face to face with my *own* mortality, I realized that I may not always be here to share our story with our children, and to teach them how they, too, can create the life of *their* dreams as well. As that letter grew to be *more* than just a letter, I realized I could potentially help more than just them.

Over the course of this book, I will teach *you* how to do the same in *your life*. I will teach you how to step into the enchanting land of make-believe to manifest a new reality, one in which magic is real, imagination is everything, and you truly *can* create Heaven on Earth.

But first, you must think happy thoughts…

> *"So come with me, where dreams are born, and time is never planned."*

PETER PAN

9

Focus

How your thoughts create reality.

PART I

fo-cus

\<noun\>

a: a center of activity, attraction, or attention.

b: a point of concentration.

Merriam Webster Dictionary

PART 1: FOCUS

"When you change the way you look at things, the
things you look at change."

MAX PLANCK,
NOBEL PRIZE WINNING PHYSICIST

A shift in perception.

That was all that I desired for my friend that day in 2019, because I knew that a simple shift in perception had the power to change everything. It had already changed everything for me, and I knew even back then, that I was just getting started.

At that point in my journey, there was no longer any doubt in my mind that we were all not only *perceiving* entirely different realities but also *creating* those perceptions. I had been experimenting and practicing with intentionally focusing on the things I desired, or what some might call the Law of Attraction, for quite a while, and I had experienced one unbelievable manifestation after another – manifestations that should *not* have been possible.

Three years prior to this phone call, my husband and I had found ourselves in an impossible situation trying to dig out from beneath a mountain of debt. We were maxed out at over $25k in credit card debt, along with a very large student loan balance, among other debts. We had no savings whatsoever, and were living paycheck to paycheck, with most of our income being spent on rent for the one-bedroom apartment we occupied in the nicest area of town. We had been in a perpetual downward spiral, adding to our debt each month just to pay for our basic living expenses, and soon found that we'd reached our limits. Credit increases were no longer available to us.

As was my typical response to anything less than ideal, I began to panic. On the other hand, my husband Kyle, the eternal optimist, seemed to be unbothered by the situation entirely. As usual, this bothered me more.

I was the one that handled our finances, and thus, had watched our debt slowly, but painstakingly compound for years, as it had become increasingly alarming and frustrating for me. Whereas Kyle, who barely paid attention to my occasional updates, had seen it more as just a bump in the road, something that would work itself out in time.

I tried to explain to him that we didn't *have* time, that we couldn't even afford groceries for the week. To this he'd responded nonchalantly, "We'll figure it out," just as he always did when I told him that our world was coming apart at the seams.

But this time he was right – we *would* figure it out. Less than one year later, we would experience our first massive quantum leap. As if we'd stumbled onto a parallel Universe, we would suddenly find ourselves in an upside-down reality, one in which we were financially stable, had a nice-sized savings account, had paid off all of our credit card debt, and were living in our dream home – a home that we didn't rent, but *owned*.

And it all started with the creation of my very first vision board.

Now, don't get me wrong, I didn't just slap a picture of a house and some cash on a piece of paper and – *voila!* – all of our dreams came true. This is not *that* kind of book. There was *absolutely* action on our part needed. In full transparency, some might even call it *massive* action. But I'd be remiss not to share that creating that vision board was in fact the catalyst that set the entire chain of events into action.

The pictures on that vision board staring back at me each day consistently brought my attention back to my hopes and dreams, and sparked one hit of inspiration after another. Inspiration that led to action that then – and this is where it gets interesting – led to events that spiraled out of my control in the most effortless and synchronistic ways to bring those visions to life.

Here's how it happened…

One afternoon, I sat at my desk racking my brain over which co-worker I could call to ask a silly question. It was a question I should know the answer to, but I needed a sanity check to be sure.

Since I worked remotely from home, I couldn't just pop my head into a co-worker's office and it felt intrusive to call and interrupt someone when I couldn't directly see if they were busy or not. So, there I'd sat wasting time, trying to get up the nerve to dial. I crossed my fingers, hoping I'd get through to someone who could actually help me.

I often had this dilemma since our office manager didn't have experience in our line of work and only handled HR functions. This meant we only had one person to go to with our questions, the managing partner of the firm, who was incessantly busy, not to mention difficult to get ahold of. Most of us also preferred *not* to commit career suicide by bothering her with basic questions, so we relied on each other's expertise as much as possible.

If only there was someone designated to handle these kinds of questions, I'd thought, frustrated. It was a thought I had no doubt had many times over the years, but this time, in the very moment that it popped into my head, one of the pictures on my vision board of a stylish and professionally dressed career woman under the words "Lady Boss" jumped out at me.

It dawned on me that it was *me* – *I* could be that person. I'd been in my position for several years and knew the rules and regulations of our industry and the policies and procedures of our company well. No one had all of the answers, of course, but I could certainly be the person to field those calls and help people get the answers they needed.

It made me think about how much we also desperately needed someone to train the new hires. We had been experiencing constant turnover for years, which only created more work for all of us. The reason why was obvious. People needed a one-stop call, a friendly face to help them through the learning curve that everyone experiences when starting at a new company.

As the training and development specialist, I could create materials and resources that outlined procedures and I could plan training sessions to share the information learned. We could *all* benefit from this in an exponential way, making it well worth the additional salary it would take to put someone in this position. Plus, it would free-up more of the managing partner's time, which was incredibly valuable and over-utilized.

What once may have just been a fleeting thought covered up immediately by my ever-growing to-do list, or whatever fire needed to be put out next, became one that my mind consistently returned to time and time again as the picture sitting on my desk became a representation of an idea. The idea took root in my mind, becoming stronger and more detailed, growing branches and leaves, each and every time my eyes inevitably landed on it.

For months the "Lady Boss" picture caught my eye, as if calling me to action. I finally got tired of the thoughts rolling around in my head and decided to put them down on paper. I put together a proposal for my boss intended to influence her to create a training and development position at work, one in which I detailed *myself* as the perfect candidate.

I received the promotion I asked for, along with a huge pay increase, and became a "boss" at work, just as depicted on my vision board.

The jar of cash on the board kept catching my eye as well, prompting many brainstorming sessions on how we could get more cash flow into our lives. I eventually decided to apply for a waitressing job. Since we were deeply in debt, we weren't doing anything in the evenings or on the weekends anyway, and it dawned on me that a side hustle might be the best way forward.

I secured a waitressing position easily, and the extra cash I was making each night became our spending money, allowing us to put more money toward our credit card debt each month.

During this time, I also was inspired to convince Kyle to start looking for a new job. I helped him get his resume in order and began applying to job postings for him that I thought he might like. He ended up accepting a job offer that paid much better than what he had been making.

With the additional income from Kyle's new job, my new position at work, and my side gig, which literally put cash in my pocket several nights a week, it was as if I'd fulfilled another one of the visions on my board – the jar of cash.

Finally, as I looked longingly each day at the beautiful house and the words "Dream Home" on the board, I decided to download real estate apps and to contact a realtor. We were nowhere close to being able to afford to buy a home and had no business wasting a realtor's time. But the vision board called to me, grabbing at my attention every moment of every day, so I did it anyway.

Kyle saw my increasing interest in real estate as an imminent sign and as if on cue, began telling everyone we knew that we were going to buy our first home. Eyes wide, I'd nod slowly in agreement, a smile plastered on my face, knowing good and well that we couldn't *really* afford to buy a house. Of course, when I told him it bothered me for him to share this information with people since I didn't believe it to be true, he looked at me like I had three heads.

In typical Kyle logic he'd stated, "But we *are* looking at houses. And we *are* going to buy one. Whether that's now or a year from now, or *three* years from now, what does that matter? No one needs to know our exact timeline. *We* don't even know our exact timeline. Seriously, Kim. Nobody cares."

In a way, I knew he was right (although I didn't care to ever admit that to him). It was my own insecurities that made it feel like we were lying to people. And with each person he told, I got less embarrassed and more comfortable with the idea. It also prompted people to begin sharing their advice with us and we learned more about the process, which we admittedly knew nothing about. We soon learned that we weren't actually *that* far off from being able to buy a home. People did it all the time, even with little to no money down. Soon, I actually started believing that we *were* ready to buy our first home.

All of these inspired actions certainly got the ball rolling in the direction of our dreams. But while these actions were incremental in their overall effect, certain events that were completely out of our control followed, and quantum leapt us forward into an entirely new reality. It appeared as though once we'd made the decision that we were going to uplevel our finances and buy a home, and got a little momentum moving in the direction of those goals, the means – which had been there all along, as if it was just waiting on us to decide – presented itself to us.

Upon hearing the news that we were looking into buying our first home, a total of $25k was gifted to us from the culmination of three unexpected sources, without us asking a single person for help. A debt consolidation plan at an extremely low interest rate landed in our lap, offered to us without us having even looked into such a thing. And a home that was way out of our league, not to mention out of our price range, became ours through a string of coincidental events.

I should have never even *seen* the home based on our price filters. As a strategy to generate more foot traffic at the open house and incite a bidding war that would drive up the price of the home, the sellers had listed it just shy of what it was actually worth.

So, there it was, right there in my inbox – this gorgeous home on the east side, with a picturesque view of the neighborhood lake, inhabited by geese and ducks and a blue heron. It had an outdoor covered spa along with a charming rock pond in the backyard full of bright orange koi fish. The inside was modern and elegant, with curated details and elaborate fixtures. It was, at that time, a dream home for us – something that we never thought could possibly be within our reach. It blew every other house in our price range away.

I'd called my realtor right away, but she confirmed that the house would go for more than the listing price, which unfortunately was already right at the top of our price point. I decided not to torture myself by going to the open house.

Then I got a text message from my sister, Dana. "Have you seen this one? I love it! Open house this Sunday. LET'S GO!" Dana loved any kind of shopping, so when she'd heard we were in the market to buy a house, she'd taken it upon herself to shop as well, specifically for homes within a short distance of her own. This one was only seven minutes away, and she would not take no for an answer. I reluctantly agreed and, as expected, we fell in love with it. Also as expected, a bidding war ensued. We did decide to make a higher offer, but the home ended up selling for more than we could afford.

We didn't get our dream home. And we were devastated.

Several weeks later, we got a call from our real estate agent. The buyers had fallen out at the last minute and the sellers didn't want to have to re-list the house and go through more showings and open houses. They were going down the list of people who had made offers and we were next on the list. We ended up getting our dream home at a price within our budget.

It felt like a miracle at the time, *the first of many*.

At the time of this conversation with my best friend in 2019, I had also already manifested what will always be one of my (two) greatest creations, my son, Knox Ryan Littrell. I had put on that same vision board that I'd made in 2016, a picture of an adorable little boy dressed in a cute, fuzzy bear suit with little ears on the hood. He had the cutest little chubby cheeks and a big smile on his face.

Two years after putting that picture on my vision board, my son was born. My mom, *who had never seen the vision board*, gifted him a fuzzy bear suit with little ears on the hood.

It wasn't until much later, when I was looking at a photo I had snapped of my son in that bear suit, that it dawned on me. I rooted through old papers and files until I'd found that long forgotten vision board from years earlier. My son wore the same bear suit from the picture, the same color, with the same pattern underneath the hood. It was the exact one from the picture! More impressive though, was the uncanny resemblance between my son and the boy in the photo. They quite literally could have been twins.

In another lovely synchronicity, due to a onesie my son wore as a newborn that had a picture of a dinosaur and the word "ROAR" on it, Kyle had taken to saying "Roar!" back to my son anytime he cried. This always made me laugh and quickly caught on, becoming our default response to his cries. We often followed up with some form of the phrase, "But isn't it such a cute roar!"

I went back to find the original picture of the little boy in the cute fuzzy bear suit on Pinterest sometime later as I only had a printed copy on my vision board. When I came across it, guess what the caption read? "The cutest Rawr! ever."

Almost everything I had placed on that vision board in 2016 ended up coming to fruition in one way or another. Some of the details so distinct, so profound, and so out of my control, that I couldn't help but imagine some kind of magic was occurring. But while the *how* and the *why*, at that time, were still very much a mystery to me, I'd seen enough proof by that phone call in 2019 to know, without a doubt, that manifestation was real. And I knew if I could manifest everything that I had from that vision board in such a short amount of time as easily as I did, I could manifest *anything*.

Thus, when I'd said out loud to my friend that I thought I'd be a millionaire one day, *I meant it*. In truth, I *already was* a millionaire in my mind – I was already looking at million-dollar homes and putting together my millionaire wardrobe. As I saw it, reality was just taking a little bit of time to catch up with me.

This is how all manifestation starts after all – it starts in the mind. It is the creation of an idea that begins the entire process. And once you learn to create ideas based on what you want, rather than what you *don't* want (which is unfortunately where most people unintentionally create from), you are well on your way to being able to manifest *anything* you can dream up.

Manifesting is a simple process. As a matter of fact, it's easy. It's merely the *mindset* that takes a bit of work. Taking control of your mind requires an intense focus, and in a world constantly vying for your attention, this can prove to be an especially difficult task. But once you understand how the mind works, you are well on your way to mastering it.

Vision Board, 2016

Photo of Boy from Vision Board

Knox and Kyle

LESSONS ON FOCUS

"Everything is Energy and that is all there is to it.
Match the frequency of the reality you want and you
cannot help but get that reality. It can be no other way.
This is not philosophy. This is physics."

OFTEN ATTRIBUTED TO ALBERT EINSTEIN

Nothing Is as It Seems

To lay the foundation for everything you are about to learn, the most important concept you must understand is this: Everything is Energy. *Absolutely everything.*

E=mc2 proves that mass and energy are interchangeable, two different forms of the same thing. Therefore, nothing you see in the world around you is definitively solid.

At the quantum level, even smaller than the atom, are tiny vibrating particles called subatomic particles which make up every single thing in the Universe. You, your dog, the fence post, each blade of grass, the food you eat, the stars in the sky, the car you drive – it is *all* made up of the same thing.

These particles are constantly rearranging themselves and shape shifting into different forms to create the tangible objects you can see and touch all around you. While it may appear that many of these objects are made up of matter, at their very core, they are but mere energy. And this energy acts in *very peculiar ways.*

Allow me to introduce you to the wonky world of Quantum Physics, where everything we *think* we know about how the world works gets tossed out the window. At the subatomic level, there is an entirely different world to the one in which we see. There is a randomness and unpredictability at play that is far

21

more interesting than that which meets the eye.

This is a world that is limitless, one that defies our laws of logic and certainly defies all laws of the physical world in which we believe that we live. For example, at the quantum level, it is entirely possible for particles to be in more than one place at a time, as in *quantum superposition*, or to be in more than one physical state at a time, as in *wave-particle duality*. It is possible for one of these particles to communicate with and instantly influence another particle that is far away, as in *quantum entanglement*. And, it is even possible for one of these particles to go right through an object, without ever making contact with it, as in *quantum tunneling*.

While these concepts may seem like something you could only find at the Hogwarts School of Witchcraft and Wizardry, it is, in fact, cutting-edge, mainstream science. But why is this important and what does it all mean for you?

What it means is that the building blocks that make up everything in the Universe, including *you*, are full of an infinite number of possibilities, so strange in their potential, one could more easily explain it as *magic*.

So, channel your inner Harry Potter, find platform nine and three quarters, and hold on tight to your wand, because the world, as you *think* you know it, is about to expand.

The Observer Effect

Of all the maddeningly strange concepts at play in quantum physics, there is one, the observer effect, that is particularly mind blowing. The double slit experiment proved that subatomic particles, upon observation, change their physical state, their behavior, and outcome in space and time. Just as *you* act differently when you know that you are being observed, so do subatomic particles.

Until they are observed, they are limitless in their capacity. A wave of potentiality is formed, meaning the particle is neither here, nor there. It is nowhere and everywhere, nothing and everything, all at the same time – it is pure energy. It is not until it is directly observed that it collapses into a state of apparent solidarity and becomes localized as a space-time event.

As the whole Universe is made up of these same subatomic particles, this means that this is how the *entire* world exists around you when you are not paying attention to it. Nothing is solid until our focus, as the observer, makes it so. In simple terms, things aren't what they are until you see them that way.

This is as true of the particles that make up the shape-shifting clouds in the sky, as it is of those that make up the seemingly solid, wooden desk that you sit at. Perhaps most importantly, it is true of *you*.

Humor me, if you will, while I take you through a tiny science experiment. Hold your hand up and extend it out in front of your face. Look at your hand.

Your hand is a solid object, is it not? It is in a definite place in space and time.

Now, look at the wall just directly behind your hand. What happens to your hand when you remove your focus from it? You may notice that in your peripheral vision, it now appears as if your hand is moving slightly. It is as if it is in more than one place at a time.

This is how each subatomic particle that makes up your hand works – until directly observed, they can be in several places at once, because your focus has not yet made them solid. Is it *here* or is it *there*? It is actually both and neither. It is in a state of *energetic possibility*.

Many quantum physics' theories allude to the fact that there are an infinite number of possibilities and potentials in the world around us – yes, *infinite*. That means that these subatomic particles can come together to quite literally create *anything*. It is the same subatomic particles that make up an old, broken down, beat-up car as it is that make up a brand new, shiny, Ferrari.

Therefore, it begs the question, how do subatomic particles choose? There is no straightforward answer to this yet, but quantum physics tells us that nothing comes into existence without first being observed. This means that the human mind plays a very pivotal role in reality.

So, perhaps the question is better answered by *you*, the observer. What are you choosing to observe, to focus on and give your attention to? Is it the things you *want* to see in your external reality, or is it the things you *don't* want to see? Is it your likes, your blessings, your hopes, and your dreams? Or is it your dislikes, your problems, your worries, and your fears? What is your focus seeking out in the world around you?

Your focus is what brings the tangible into existence. It is what plucks mere possibilities out of the ether and places them right in front of your nose. It is even what takes the ideas out of your head and brings them to fruition. It is what creates the world, as you perceive it, around you. This is why every person's perception of reality is entirely different, because it is being created every single moment by our focus.

You will come to find that focusing on a problem *never* solves the problem. It only *solidifies* it. But, when you remove your focus from a problem, it then has the ability to shape shift, sometimes even disappearing altogether. Focusing on solutions requires an entirely different mindset. And a focus on *solutions* is what *creates* the ability to perceive the solution itself.

The Reticular Activating System

Allow me to bring this concept down from the clouds and into the physical world that we live in. After all, we don't live in our minds, *right*? There *is* a physical here and now created by collective consciousness. And life would appear to be going on all around us, with or without, our focus. As we are constantly scanning the world around us, it would seem to be inadvertent what our eyes land on, or our ears hear, and what our thoughts are then interpreting.

This is because consciously it *is* seemingly incidental, but the process starts long before the conscious. It starts in the subconscious, with something called the Reticular Activating System. The RAS, for short, sits at the base of our brain, and serves a very important function. It acts as the gatekeeper to our conscious mind, filtering and prioritizing sensory information. Its job is to help us focus on relevant stimuli while ignoring the irrelevant.

Our eyes alone are capable of processing ten million bits of information to the brain every second – and that's just *one* of our senses. As you can imagine, if our brains were required to consciously download and interpret every single bit of information as it was occurring around us, we wouldn't be able to focus on anything! To prevent overload, our RAS filters through the data to determine which bits and pieces to allow passageway into our conscious minds.

There are two categories of data our RAS deems relevant to us. First, anything that will warn us of danger, in an attempt to keep us and our offspring safe in order to ensure our survival. And second, anything that it deems important to us based on whether or not it is in harmony with our dominant thoughts. In other words, what we think about *the most*.

The latter is where things get interesting and where the Law of Attraction comes into play. By focusing our thoughts on something we are telling our brains what to seek out in the world around us. And when we tell our brains to look for something, like a dog sniffing out a bone, it is relentless in its pursuit. The blinders automatically go up to ignore anything in opposition to what we have told it to look for, creating a sort of tunnel vision upon our request.

You may have seen The Gorilla Experiment, a popular video that has made its rounds on social media. Harvard University students asked a group of people to watch a short video in which six people, three in white shirts and three in black shirts, pass basketballs back and forth to each other. The observers were asked to keep count of the number of passes made by those in white shirts. In the middle of the video, a person in a gorilla costume walks into the middle of the screen and thumps its chest for several seconds.

The experiment asked, how many of the people who were focused on the number of passes by people in white shirts noticed the black gorilla? Turns out that despite the gorilla's overwhelming presence right in front of the camera, more than half of the people in the audience completely missed it, never even noticing it at all! "What gorilla?" They'd cried, surprised. When they watched the video back, now *looking* for the gorilla, they were shocked at how they could have possibly missed it.

What does this tell you? It proves that if you are not focused on something, you may not ever notice its existence, even if it is right in front of you. This is especially true if you are looking for something in opposition to it – in this case, white shirts being opposite in color to a black gorilla.

This is your RAS hard at work, filtering through millions of bits of data going on all around you every single second and only giving you access to what it thinks you want to observe – as determined by *you*.

This is why it is so important to get *clear* on your desires, to write them down, and to bring your attention back to your goals often. This is how you train your brain to look for the opportunities, for those *potentials* – which let me remind you, are *infinite* – in the world around you.

If you still have doubts, take a look at another study conducted at Harvard in an MBA class in which they surveyed students to find that 97% of the graduating class either did not have specific goals or, at least, hadn't written their goals down on paper.

Years later, when they reached out to those students, they learned that the 3% that had written down their goals at the time of graduation were making *ten times* more money than the other 97% *combined*. Take a second to let that sink in – 3% of students were making more than *all* of the other 97% added together.

Incredible, right? That's the power of specificity on the brain. Tell it what opportunities to look for and it will go to work to find them.

You may have heard the advice to get clear on what you want in a partner by writing down the specific characteristics and traits that you desire for them to have. There are many stories of people meeting their significant other after doing so, and that person being eerily similar to the details that they had written down. While this may appear to be some kind of black magic, it's actually just your RAS hard at work.

Let's take a look at two drastically different sets of dominant thoughts, or *focus*, on the same topic – one *problem*-oriented and one *solution*-oriented – to see this in action.

In scenario number one, you have come to a place in life where you have decided you are ready to find your wife. You are tired of dating around and you want to meet someone who is adventurous and wants to travel the world with you, before settling down and starting a family. Although you haven't found her yet, you believe your wife is out there waiting for you. You think of your wife often, daydreaming about her, and looking for her everywhere you go.

You sit down at a restaurant for lunch with a friend, and your RAS is busy filtering out millions of bits of data all around you, so that your conscious mind can focus on the conversation at hand. But during your conversation, you overhear another voice, even though it's a few tables away. Your attention is drawn to an attractive woman talking to her friend. You hear her say, "I just want someone who wants to travel and go on adventures with me!"

Your RAS, while filtering through the sounds of conversations at all the tables around you, allowed the sound of her voice through because it deemed it to be important, or of interest to you. Thanks to your RAS, you may have just found your soulmate!

Now, let's take a look at scenario number two.

You have gone on several bad dates, and you've determined that every woman just wants to settle down and have kids right away. What you want, someone to travel with and have adventures with, simply isn't out there. You don't even think about your wife, only the *lack* of women that want the same things that you want.

You go to that same restaurant, and even though the love of your life is just a few tables away, you never even notice her. Your RAS filtered her out of your consciousness because she was not in harmony with your dominant thoughts. Perhaps you instead noticed all of the families with children, and all of the pregnant women, since that is what you predominantly think about.

The more you focus on a person, a place, a thing, or an idea, the more likely you are to pick out the potentials for it in your external environment, for better or for worse.

This is the reason why a coin collector notices coins everywhere they go, while others may not even register them. It is why you start seeing a particular type of car everywhere after you decide it is the car you want to buy. It is the reason why (and this is important) practicing gratitude every day has you finding more and more reasons to be grateful. It is the reason why one's to-do list may never seem to end, because a continued focus on it tells the brain to keep looking for things that need to be done. It is the reason why some people seem to always have such good luck, while drama seems to follow others. It is the reason why an exciting opportunity lands in your lap after you decide you are going to start focusing on your job search. And it is also the reason why a spilled coffee in the morning creates a day full of mishaps, because focus remained on that spilled coffee, finding more and more potentials throughout the day to align with that focus.

For better or for worse, your attention is drawn to whatever your mind is predominantly focused on. And in a world of infinite potentials and possibilities, this can be truly magical. Unfortunately, if left uncontrolled, it can also be disastrous.

The Conscious Consumer

I'll say it again, your focus is powerful. It creates the world, as you perceive it, around you. And yet, rather than being intentional about our focus, most of us choose to give our control away every second of every day. Often, before even having our first sip of coffee in the morning.

Rather than being proactive about our mornings and allowing for quiet, open, creative space to formulate our own thoughts and ideas, to focus our attention on our intentions for our day ahead, or to meditate or journal to find clarity, many choose to immediately dispel the quiet. We introduce outside influence and throw ourselves into a reactive state first thing in the morning.

There is the most common, automatic reach for a cell phone to scroll through social media, or online news, sports, or gossip sources. Some will check their emails or their work calendars. Others may turn on the television or the radio to hear the familiar voices of their favorite strangers debating over inane topics or sharing the political shortfalls, and often tragic news, of the day prior.

We allow ourselves to be led down one rabbit hole after another. We get excited, upset, even outraged about things that are not even particularly important to us, information and ideas that often have very little effect, to no relevance, on our own lives whatsoever. Sometimes we find out later that the information wasn't even true or had been taken significantly out of context. But the damage has already been done.

This morning routine unsurprisingly leads to a day full of chaos and stress. The pattern of consuming and reacting, and prioritizing external influence over our own internal focus continues, creating a snowball effect on our mind, our day, and ultimately, our life.

Most people have absolutely no idea that their mind is being controlled. One might imagine some maniacal figure, deviously laughing as he plots to take over the world, one mind at a time. I wish it were that simple, at least then there would be someone to blame, other than ourselves.

But the truth is, that while our mind is one of our most precious resources, we hand over the controls willingly, typically to the highest bidder. Advertisements, marketing and political campaigns, click bait, sensationalism for ratings, dopamine hits for likes, outrageous gossip – it is *all* intended to capture and hold our attention hostage. We are locked in, our minds frantically chewing on one sound bite after another. It is like being on a never-ending hamster wheel of over-stimulation that is designed to keep us consumed with everything *except* the betterment of our own lives.

And as our focus is hijacked, and our thoughts handed to us on a silver platter, the world we see around us is not of our creation, but rather *being created* by something outside of us. As one thought leads to another, which leads to another, we are creating more and more of the same by default, haphazardly and unintentionally. We are telling our brains what to look for based on what we are thinking about the most, which is heavily influenced by what we are *consuming* the most. This would not necessarily be such a bad thing, if what we were consuming was not a constant stream of negativity, drama, tragedy, and horror.

So, how do you put a stop to this? How do you change the algorithm for what you see next? How do you take back control of your mind and your life? You must start by becoming intentional about what you do, *and do not*, consume.

As I write this, it is the year 2022 and we are coming off the tail-end of the Covid-19 pandemic, an outbreak that rocked the entire world. Government shutdowns, shelter in place orders, families being ripped apart, and sickness and death have consumed our lives for almost two years.

As the Pandemic slowly spread from one country to another and then, very quickly, each of our backyards, mass hysteria and pure and utter chaos ensued. Media outlets began reporting breaking news as the facts came out. Facts that were in fact, *not* fact, at all. Misinformation spread like wildfire from trusted sources, and it soon became obvious that no one knew anything for sure.

Yet, like addicts, we scrolled feverishly through online sources and social media to get our fix, clicking on every sensational and misleading headline that came our way. We tuned into the news morning and night, anxiously awaiting the next update, our eyes glued to our television sets, the death count figure on the screen rising every second.

We argued over what was true, or right, or helpful, and what was not. People began lashing out at each other looking for someone to blame. The negativity spread almost as quickly as Covid-19 had, with each of us in our own way, adding to the momentum of the narrative that the world was coming to an end.

I remember looking down at my glass of wine in the summer of 2020, half drunk in the middle of the day, in the middle of the week, acne covering my face, and ten pounds heavier than I had been at the start of the pandemic. My mind felt frantic, unable to determine what it was that I should do next, as I listened to the governor on the television in the background talking about the latest restrictions in my state.

I'd picked up my phone to scroll for the one hundredth time that day when I heard my son's frustrated cry break into my awareness. Snapping to, I'd wondered, how long had he been crying for me? He'd gotten so whiny lately that I'd learned to block it out. But it was in that moment that I realized he had become excessively whiny *because* I had been blocking him out. I hadn't been focused on him at all, but rather focused only on the tiny device in my hands and the screen on my wall, as if transported to some other reality, ignoring his pleas for my attention day after day.

What kind of mother had I become? And who was this person who was so unhealthy and such a mess, drinking in the middle of the day? It was then that I realized my focus had been hijacked. I had been so worried about the Covid-19 outbreak that I had sought out ways to make myself another kind of sick. And it wasn't just me – I looked around and saw that everyone was similarly being affected.

As human contact and fresh air dwindled, a shadow pandemic seemed to be following closely along on Covid-19's heels; A pandemic of perhaps just as much magnitude – the symptoms of which were varying degrees of addiction and depression, stress, anxiety, frustration, and anger. Some combination of these seemed to have a chokehold on everyone I knew.

The most paralyzing fear possible – the fear of *causing death* – had grabbed ahold of our minds. We had allowed ourselves to be led into a state of panic and stress day after day, for months on end. And as a result, our brains and bodies did what they were designed to do.

The prefrontal cortex, or the creative and critical thinking centers of our brains, shut down as our amygdala's took over, alerting our nervous system of imminent danger. Blood flowed from our brains to our arms and legs, readying us for fight or flight. Tunnel vision set in and our blinders went up to anything non-Covid related, so that we could stay hyper-focused on the perceived threat. No one could see the forest through the trees, the full picture gone completely from our awareness, as we zoomed in on the monster that was Covid-19. We settled into a never-ending stress-response, as our bodies prepared for survival.

Many chose flight as they retracted from life completely, dulling their senses with some form of escape, while others had chosen to fight. Without access to our rational minds, *no one* got any smarter. It was clear what the constant negativity, fear, and worry was doing to people, *including me*, and it had spiraled out of control with far too much momentum.

Kyle and I came together in the awareness that we not only needed to protect our family from sickness, but also needed to protect our minds from sickness as well. We made the decision that we had done all we could do to prepare and to protect ourselves from Covid-19, and that now the best thing we could do for our family was *tune out*. We turned off the news, turned off our social media notifications, and removed ourselves from the Covid conversation entirely. Many of our well-meaning family members and friends had become addicted to the fear, and constant drama, and negativity. We decided if we couldn't change the conversation, we simply would not be a part of it any longer.

Once we made the decision and took the first few necessary steps to remove ourselves from the constant Covid narrative, the frantic energy stopped. It was quiet again, and our focus returned to the things that we truly cared about. Once we stopped consuming, commiserating, and contributing to it, we were able to again see past it all – to see the big picture. We focused in on the positives in our lives instead, again looking to the dreams for the future we had up ahead.

We counted our blessings. We realized that we had a unique opportunity to spend more time with our son and to focus on our little family, to read more, to cook more, and to work on projects that we otherwise wouldn't have had the time for. By focusing on these blessings, we had told our brains to look for more blessings. It was as though our blinders went up yet again, but this time to anything Covid *related*, and we were suddenly unaffected by it.

Although the pandemic continued to occur at the same potency in our shared world, by choosing to tune it out, we had essentially changed the frequency of, or changed the channel, on our thoughts. And thus, we heard a new tune. We saw a new picture. We read a new story. We began perceiving an entirely different reality than all those around us.

There was a new energy that we seemed to have tapped into. We suddenly had crystal clear clarity. A lightness had returned to our step, as though we'd somehow found a way to float above it all. We could still see the people down below – the thick canopy of storm clouds that covered them, the darkness and the stifling, muggy air as they gasped for breath, could still see the mud they waded through, thick as quicksand, pulling them down deeper the more they struggled against it.

For a time, we tried to reach out to them, to pull them up into the cool, clean air, to bring them with us. But it was as though our words just bounced back, unheard entirely, as if we were trying to communicate from another dimension.

Our world seemed to have been torn into two vastly different realities. In one, we found more calm, more silver linings, more and more reasons to be positive and grateful. Our lives began to flourish. We found more joy, more passion and love, more freedom, more opportunity, and as you will soon learn, more success – *success beyond our wildest dreams.*

Whereas, in what would seem to be an entirely different world, there were those who found more doom and gloom. The more they consumed it, the more they looked for it, the more they rooted it out. Even when the pandemic began to taper off and the world went back to business as usual, many were never able to fully reset their nervous systems. Those who had leaned into the negativity, allowing it to consume them, continued to find more reasons to be negative. They found more reasons to be fearful or to be angry. And once Covid-19 had, for all intents and purposes, disappeared, they *still* continued to find more sickness, and devastation, and ruin all around them.

I use this example not to downplay the monstrosity that was Covid-19, nor to suggest that anyone that experienced loss or hardship during its reign of terror were in any way responsible. I have no doubt that everyone's experience was very different – that we were lucky to have been able to put our blinders up and be seemingly so unaffected by it. Nonetheless, this is an example on a very grand scale how much power you have over your own focus.

It is meant to show that even when the entire world is consumed, you still have a choice. You still get to decide where you put your focus, or where you *do not* put your focus. No one, and no event or circumstance, can take that power away from you…unless you allow it. You are in control of your mind, always.

The great stoic philosophers of the 3rd century understood this in a way that many people today still do not. Take a page from stoicism and the great Marcus Aurelius, who once said, "You have power over your mind – not outside events. Realize this, and you will find strength."

While you cannot stop the inevitable pull on your focus from all things external, you can always course correct. You can always choose not to engage. You can always choose to change the channel, to put your focus elsewhere. You can always choose to perceive things differently.

Use this monumental example to serve as proof that you do not have to tune in to all of the popular everyday things that you think you need to – like the horrific series on television that everyone is talking about, or the gruesome true crime podcast that is all the rave. The more shocking or disturbing something is, the more your brain will chew on it. Your mind isn't just consumed while watching it, as those scenes will seep into your subconscious and will play out over and over and over again each time something reminds you of them.

You do not have to be up to date on all of the pop culture and gossip hitting the headlines. You do not have to tune into the news, or rather, what *passes* as the news, to stay up to date on all of the tragic and alarming current events as they unfold. Creating controversy, ringing the alarms, and scaring the hell out of people are what bring viewership and ratings. Don't buy into it. Don't let it darken your perception of the world. Don't let it *create* your world.

It will never make one bit of a difference whether you know all the details of the most recent tragedy that we call a current event. Spoiler alert, once everyone has gotten upset, angry, and hurt, and argued over what to do about it (while actually never doing anything), there will be another tragedy within just a few weeks to months. This tragedy will become more current, and thus, the new topic of conversation, while the old one is forgotten completely.

If you want to change the world, change yourself. Stop feeding into the craziness. As one kid shoots up a school and an entire nation's focus is consumed with it, becoming the topic of conversation at every dinner table in America, five more kids get a similar idea. *Change the conversation.*

You can hold space for the suffering, you can feel empathy for those who have experienced tragedy, and you can even offer physical or financial assistance without becoming consumed with it. You don't need to know every detail. You don't need to talk about it until you are blue in the face. And you certainly don't need to be reminded of it every time you turn on your television. You don't need to be *that* informed of all of the bad things happening in the world. Look for the good. Spread the good. *Change the conversation.*

If you are worried about becoming uninformed when you stop watching the news or delete your social media apps, ask yourself, uninformed about *what*, exactly? Yet a better question would be, what do you want to be informed about *instead?* Because for every *no* there is a *yes*, and for every *yes* there is a *no*. And if you are spending time watching the news, it means you are *not* spending time thinking about, listening to, or watching something that can better your life.

When you have a moment of awkwardness because the small talk is about the latest news event that you know nothing about, stand tall and remember that just because it's an important part of *their* reality, doesn't mean it has to be an important part of *yours*.

It *is* small talk after all. The only big talk in this world is that of ideas – *original* ideas. And you won't find those handed to you on a silver platter of regurgitated lines said over and over again, for weeks on end, to an entire nation of people. You may find them in books, you may find them in nature, you may even find them on the playground. But where you will not find them is on the news. Remember that fear shuts down the part of your brain where original ideas are created. Fear, quite literally, makes you dumb. Fear is, by far, *the worst F-word of them all.*

As President Franklin D. Roosevelt said in his inaugural speech in 1933, "The only thing we have to fear is fear itself." Watch what you allow to take ahold of your mind, for your mind will create more, and more, and more of whatever you allow into it. Fear begets fear.

There will always be fear and doom and gloom somewhere that you can choose to focus on. *Always*. And in duality, there will also be faith and kindness and positivity that you can choose to focus on as well. *Always*. Make your choice wisely.

You are fully responsible for your thoughts, your perception, your expectations, and the meaning you give to the things happening around you. In all situations there is bad and good, dark and light, problem and opportunity. You always have a choice in what you choose to observe.

Look for the good. Spread the good. *Change the conversation.*

Be conscious of what you choose to consume, especially on a regular basis, for it will play a huge role in the lens of perception with which you view the world. And that lens will create the potential for what you see next. It *will* create your reality.

As Stanford Professor, David Eagleman said, "Instead of reality being passively recorded by the brain, it is actively constructed by it." As stimuli is filtered to the brain from the RAS, based on your thoughts and what you think about the most, the brain's frontal lobe then interprets the stimuli and uses that interpretation to construct reality, or what some scientists refer to as a sort of hallucination. That's right, what you see around you is not real. It is only a perception. It is a representation of what your brain *thinks* is going on, and what it *predicts* will happen, based on its interpretation of past and current stimuli. You, then, perceive this representation as reality. The world you see around you is only a projection of your mind.

This is why they say, change your mind, change your life. The simplest, easiest way to change your mind is to stop paying attention to what you do not want to play out in your own life. Guard your mind like a fortress, allowing in only that which serves you. Remove any content that does not support what you desire to expand in your life, and intentionally tune in to that which does.

As Tony Robbins is known for saying, "Where focus goes, energy flows." Where do you want energy to flow? Immerse yourself in other people's stories who have accomplished the things you want to accomplish, or have created the kind of life that you want to create, and tune out the rest.

For the past ten years, I have not only intentionally set aside time and given myself space to think for myself and to create my own vision, but I have also filled the majority of my days with only content that inspires that vision. Content that has kept my dreams in the forefront of my mind, that continuously offers me proof of what is possible, and has given me the knowledge, tools, and resources to make those dreams come true. This has been a constant in my life – audiobooks and podcasts on personal development in the background every day while cooking, cleaning, running errands, working, walking, etc.

Through the sheer volume of consuming this kind of content, and the repetition of the same ideas and information over and over again, seeping into my subconscious, and making them my truth, I successfully rewired my brain, creating new neural pathways. This is called neuroplasticity, and it is how your brain goes about creating habitual behaviors, and thus, creating the self, based on its interpretation and predictions about reality.

Stories of success became the norm in my everyday life. Rags to riches became the norm. Multi-million-dollar businesses that regular people created became the norm. Wildly successful creatives, artists, and writers, who are paid handsomely for their craft, became the norm. Lives of passion and influence, abundance, fulfillment, and even ease, became the norm.

And I celebrated along with each of these stranger's stories as if they were my own, each story providing me with more and more evidence of what was possible. I allowed their success to serve as proof that if they could do it, then I could do it too. I directed all of my focus around the things I wanted by immersing myself in other people's realities that had those things already, rather than tuning into realities that were no better than my own.

By choosing this kind of content, I created my own little world within – a world where magic was real, possibilities were endless, and *everyone* made their dreams come true. And I believe because of this, all of my dreams have come true too.

What DO You Want

One of the things I say to my four-year-old son on a daily basis is "Don't think about what you *don't* want, think about what you *do* want." I'll also often say to him, "Don't *tell me* what you *don't* want. *Tell me* what you *do* want."

We'll be playing Candy Land and as he's drawing a card, he'll say "I hope I *don't* get a …". This helpful reminder will make him immediately re-think his position. He'll quickly say, "Oh, oh, I mean, I hope I *do* get a…". He'll have to stop and look at the board again to consider for the first time what it is that he actually *does* want to draw.

This is a common occurrence, as most people could give you a whole laundry list of what they *don't* want. Meanwhile, if you ask them what they *do* want, they pause to rack their brains as if it's the first time they've ever considered such a question.

You'd be surprised how often my son draws what he's thinking about, that turn or the next, whether he is thinking about what he *does* or *does not* want, which reinforces the lesson wonderfully. If this is the one and only saying of mine that sticks with him for the rest of his life, I will be immensely happy, knowing that I have given him a 30-year lead over my own understanding of the power of focus.

Mother Theresa once said, "I will never attend an anti-war rally. If you have a peace rally, invite me." She knew that if she attended a rally about war, it would be shining a spotlight on, and promoting, the very thing she *did not* want. However, if she attended a peace rally it would be promoting the thing she *did* want.

Perhaps she would have been best suited to have a conversation with our legislature about all of the "wars" they enact on our home front in the name of domestic problems. The war on drugs, the war on poverty, the war on crime, the war on terror – not only have none of these wars ever solved these issues, but they've actually gotten worse, perhaps as a result of these public policies.

Can you imagine how different the results may have been if instead of these wars on drugs, poverty, crime, and terror, there were equally momentous national policies and movements around health and wellness, financial literacy and abundance, mindset and positive thinking, meditation and peace, inclusion and kindness?

What you focus on has no choice but to expand. So, while all of the different types of cancer awareness weeks are a virtuous idea, they miss the mark entirely. Perhaps the money put toward these would be better served put toward organic, whole-foods, clean and green, health-conscious initiatives instead.

Many people who have successfully quit drinking or smoking will tell you to find something else you can do instead during the times that you would have had a drink or smoked a cigarette. Some people use gum, some use snacks (I wouldn't advise this), some have a cup of tea or a shirley temple. The idea is, if you are thinking about the new habit – *it's time to have a cup of tea* – you won't be thinking about the old habit – *It is not time to have a cigarette*.

Always remind yourself that what you resist persists. What you push against pushes right back. So rather than fighting against the old, build the new. Rather than bashing what you hate, promote what you love. Rather than focusing on removing unwanted things from your life, focus on adding in good things, until there is simply no more room for the unwanted. This switch in your mindset will make all the difference in your life.

The Law of Attraction

The Law of Attraction is a Universal philosophy that suggests that a person's thoughts are like magnets, attracting, and therefore determining, one's reality. What you think about, you bring about. As we've already seen through our discussion of the brain, this is a scientifically correct statement – not only does a person's brain construct reality, but the more you think about something, the more you are likely to notice the opportunities for it in your external environment.

Yet, there are many naysayers. Many people will tell you that they have "tried" it and have concluded that the Law of Attraction simply doesn't work. After all, if it really worked, wouldn't everyone be millionaires? That *is* what most people want, right?

Let me assure you, the Law of Attraction, much like the Law of Gravity, is always working. It may be working to your benefit, such as keeping you from falling off of the Earth's surface, or to your detriment, such as falling off of a ten-story building. Nevertheless, it is always working. Trying to *make* it work is like trying to *make* gravity work. *Pointless.* It is happening with, or without your consent, 24 hours a day, seven days a week. Your belief in it, or acceptance of it, makes absolutely no difference.

The problem here is your assumption that the Law of Attraction gives a damn about what you "want." Just like the Law of Gravity couldn't give a damn about whether or not you want to plummet to your death, the Law of Attraction is equally unconcerned and unhindered by your desires.

What you want does not come into play, only what you predominantly think about. It does not make any difference *how* you are thinking about the things you are thinking about the most – whether you are thinking about it negatively or positively – or whether you are thinking about it in regards to yourself or to other people (hot tip: this is why you should never think or speak ill of others) – it only matters that you are thinking about it *at all*. And this is where most people unfortunately go wrong.

A common misconception that people have when it comes to the Law of Attraction is thinking that the Universe, or what we will scientifically call your subconscious, can discern between what you *do* want vs. what you *don't* want based on *how* you are thinking about it. To understand what I mean by this, take away the words *do* and *don't*. What is left? Only want. It does not matter what words you put in front or behind the subject matter at hand, you are still attracting it by thinking about it at all.

I would implore you, especially if you are one of the naysayers, to take a look at your thoughts through a microscope. Unfortunately, while you may *think* you are thinking about what you *do* want, you may actually be unintentionally thinking about what you *don't* want. Many people do this without even realizing that they are doing it. I was certainly one of those people in the beginning of my manifestation journey as well.

For example, if you are having thoughts about having *no* debt or *paying off* all of your debt, that you *don't want* to be overweight, or desire *to lose* weight, that you *don't want* to get sick or *wish you weren't* sick – notice that the dominant thought revolves around debt, weight, and sickness, and therefore, that is what you are attracting and solidifying into your reality.

Change your mindset from one that is focused on lack or problems, and therefore negative (what I don't want or what I don't have), to one that is abundant or solution-oriented, and therefore positive (what I do want or what I'd like to have). By shifting the focus away from the verb (or the predicate) and onto the noun (or the subject) of the sentence, it will result in different perspectives and thought patterns.

This concept is often associated with cognitive restructuring, or cognitive-behavioral therapy, whereby altering language and thought patterns is a deliberate strategy to bring about positive changes in behavior and emotions.

For example, if you are thinking about being healthy, you will look for more ways to be healthy – you will act healthier, i.e. make a healthier choice at the grocery store. In opposition to this, if you are thinking about how unhealthy you are, you will often fulfill that bias by continuing to make unhealthy choices. *Why not* get a super-sized coke from McDonalds? You already *are* unhealthy, and a smaller size coke is certainly not going to change that!

Your thoughts determine how you show up in the world. They are self-fulfilling prophecies. If you want your thoughts to work to your benefit rather than your detriment, you must change the conversation you are having with the Universe inside of your head every single minute of every single day. You must shift the patterning of your thoughts when you are not even *thinking* about thinking.

When you find a penny on the ground, pick it up, and say a quick prayer of gratitude that money is so easy to find. You can get into the habit of saying something as simple as, "Thank you, Universe. More please."

Celebrate and express gratitude each time you get paid. When paying bills, say to yourself, "There's more where that came from." Rather than thinking about the money leaving your possession, think about how wonderful it is that you can afford what luxury that bill is providing in your life.

If it is your rent or mortgage, say to yourself, "Thank you for this roof over my head and the warmth of my cozy home." If it's your cell phone bill, "Thank you for this amazing little device that fits in my pocket and provides me with answers, directions, entertainment, and communication anytime I need it."

Whether money is flowing in or out or your possession, think these magical words, "Money flows to me freely and abundantly," and start looking for it everywhere. When you spend money, say to yourself, "Every penny I spend comes back to me ten-fold."

Intentionally focusing on thoughts such as these will begin to train your brain to think differently. Focus on abundance and gratitude and start expecting money to come to you easily, rather than always anticipating the opposite of this. Start expecting discounts at the register, checks in your mailbox rather than bills, and money on the ground everywhere you go. Start expecting that people *want* to give you money and believing that you are worthy of massive compensation.

The same concept can be used in regard to your relationships with others. If you want your partner to help out around the house more, or to stop bossing you around, or to feel more supported in any situation or relationship, you have to stop thinking about the *lack* of support that you currently feel. By focusing on the lack of what you want, you are creating a perception of reality that you do not desire. And by constantly thinking about it, you will continuously find the proof of it all around you.

Instead, look for the tiniest ways in which your partner already does help out around the house. When they put their plate in the sink instead of leaving it on the table, acknowledge it, even thank them for it. Celebrate it.

As Johanne Wolfgang von Goethe said, "Treat people as if they were what they ought to be, and you help them become what they are capable of becoming." If you want more affection or love in your relationship, start looking for it and acknowledging even the smallest ways in which you already see it. Start creating more of it by simply looking for what you want, rather than looking for what you don't want in every interaction. Do not let even the smallest gesture go by unnoticed. Increase your awareness of it and the acts themselves will increase as well.

Delightfully Delusional

Design a life in your head that you desire and then begin focusing on the details of that life. In a world where anything is possible, you must start imagining what could be, rather than trying to create from what already is. Start daydreaming because it will make you a happier person regardless of your external circumstances and you will inevitably experience better luck in your life.

But know that if you want to *actually* create the life that you dream of, it will require a complete overhaul in the way you think. You must train your brain to think differently. You must become delightfully delusional.

It was certainly delusional for me to think I was going to be a millionaire one day when my family was making just less than $100k a year with no legitimate plan to make any more than that. It was more delightful, however, to think I was going to become a millionaire, rather than thinking that I was going to stay stuck in that same reality forever, poor for the rest of my life.

So, I leaned into the more delightful thought, and became more and more delusional about it until the impossible seemed possible, until the possible became inevitable, until the inevitable became already done in my mind, and until already done actually *became* my reality. Once you *already are* a millionaire in your mind, reality will reflect it back to you. Everything you see out there is a reflection of what's inside of you. Start with the inside if you want to change the outside.

Ceremoniously putting thoughts like "I am a millionaire," into your mind several times a day while "practicing" the Law of Attraction is a great place to start. However, it is the *other* twenty-three hours and forty-five minutes of your day, when the Law of Attraction is still very much in effect, that is going to play the biggest role in constructing the world around you.

Begin looking under the hood, intentionally observing your thoughts throughout the day, and pivoting to ones that better serve you. Most people have no idea what they are actually thinking about all day long, or what those thoughts may be creating. You, too, may be surprised by what you find inside that head of yours. Odds are, the majority of your thoughts throughout the day are in direct opposition to what you actually want.

People want what they don't already have, otherwise they wouldn't want it, right? If someone wants to be rich, it's because they are likely *not* rich *now*. And that unfortunately means being broke is the reality in front of them that they are observing all day long (and likely have been observing for decades).

Therefore, they are, by default, thinking about being broke a majority of the time. It's right in front of their face, and they are reminded of it every time they look at their bank account, go shopping, accidentally spend too much money, pay a bill, or see something they want that they can't afford.

Thinking about what you are experiencing right in front of you is a signal to your subconscious to keep looking for it. And just like the subatomic particles that make up everything in the Universe, while you are focused on it, it is definite – there is no room for shapeshifting, no room for transformation.

This means that if you remain focused on being broke, thus continuing to solidify it, when you get to a point up ahead when enough time has passed that you could have had something different, you are still stuck with the same reality that you had in the past because you never took your eyes off of it. Whatever is under your focus is solid and unwavering.

When my son sees the blue space right in front of him on the Candy Land board that will make him lose a turn if his game piece lands on it, he automatically starts thinking about that blue space. But what if he just looked past the blue space and saw the rainbow trail up ahead instead?

This is where we want our focus, not on what is right in front of us, but up ahead a few spaces, on the *potential* of what we *want* to see in front of us next. By essentially ignoring the present moment and instead plucking another potential out of the ether to focus on, it is as if you are creating a future moment in time, and placing it upon your path to eventually recognize.

When people refer to quantum leaping, this is what is happening. They are so focused on what they want to see up ahead that they don't even realize time passing them by. They don't see what is right in front of them, shapeshifting and transforming into something new, because they are not paying attention to it. They have kept their focus on the idea of the scenario that they desire for so long, that before they know it, that scenario is upon them. It is as if they have drawn those circumstances to them, rather than having had to put in extreme effort and time to get to that future reality.

Let me be clear about this. This is not about seeing something that is *not* there. It is about seeing what *actually is* there. You must begin seeing things as they are in their natural form – energy, not matter. Everything you see around you is an energetic representation of what your thoughts have created up to this point. But energy is not standing still. It is constantly flowing, constantly moving. If you are viewing what is right in front of your eyes as concrete, it is only your observation of it that is making it appear that way. Generate new thoughts to embody a new energy and create something new.

The Universe is abundant and constantly expanding. Remember, quantum physics points to the truth that the Universe is infinite and that all potentials exist, so the potential for the things that you desire are already there – this is just simply about allowing yourself to perceive them.

This will require a deliberate intentionality at first. It will take an extreme amount of awareness, effort, and perseverance to change your focus, and thus the direction of your energy. It's not easy to look past your current reality for the potential reality of what you want. But that is what is required of you, not just some of the time when you are "practicing" the law of attraction, but at a higher frequency than you are witnessing your current reality.

Thanks to neural plasticity, it won't always be this hard or this intentional. The practice of observing your thoughts, creating new thoughts, and the nature of the thoughts themselves, will soon become habitual. You will hardly have to think about it at all. Increase the frequency with which you practice being delightfully delusional until it becomes second nature, until it *is* your frequency, and has simply become a part of who you are.

As Nikola Tesla once said, "If you want to find the secrets of the Universe, think in terms of energy, frequency, and vibration." At your core, you are mere energy, and your vibration is determined by the frequency of your thoughts. The more frequently you are thinking about something, the higher the resonance, the more you match up to that thing, and the more you draw it into your magnetic field. Just like a magnet, you will begin attracting more and more of what you want. Soon enough, your delight will no longer be so delusional.

Create New Memories

If you are no longer thinking about what you *don't* want, you are focused on what you *do* want, and you are doing it at a high enough frequency, yet you still have not attracted everything you desire then I say, *hold steady, my friend.*

You are attempting to counteract a *lifetime* of thinking about what you don't want, and while manifestation absolutely has the ability to occur instantly, our observation of the 3D reality in which we live sometimes takes a little time and space to manifest. This is especially true if memories of your past experiences keep popping up and getting in the way of your quantum leap. You may need to go back in time and change those past experiences to serve the new reality you are summoning forth. Don't worry, you don't need a DeLorean or a mad scientist to do this. All you need is an open mind and a willingness to, again, *see things differently.*

The past is an interesting concept. We believe the past to be stuck in time, in this place that we cannot touch and can have no influence over now. We view it as this solid thing that cannot transform or shapeshift.

But isn't it interesting how memories fade, the details becoming less defined when we've not recalled them for a while? Isn't it interesting how some memories leave us completely, while others take on a mind of their own, growing and evolving into great stories that maybe never even actually happened just as we remember?

How confusing it can be when you've added a little bit of drama to make for a good story – a little embellishment here, and a little enhancement there. What *actually* happened? One may never know for sure once a story has been told over and over again in a certain way. This is how legends are born. It is also how limitations, boundaries, and constraints are woven into personal identities.

According to Albert Einstein, arguably the greatest mind of all time, the past does not exist, and time, as a whole, is not even real. *Um, what?* Before you short circuit on this idea, consider this question: If everyone is observing a different reality, and no two people's observation is exactly the same, are the events of the past real? Or are they simply mind-made illusions, unique to every single person walking the Earth, being created by thoughts in the now?

If our past experiences are simply illusions, created and held only within our mind, are they stuck, unmoving, and unwavering, in time? Or do we have the ability to alter them now, based on a new observation of them, a new perception – to move them around, to adjust them to better suit us? Better yet, rather than fighting the old memory, could we just let it go completely, and build entirely new memories in time that serve us more?

We don't remember every single thing that has happened in our lives. It would be impossible to do so. According to psychological studies, we only remember about 25% of our past experiences, at best. The things we do remember, we typically recall because we had an emotional response to the event. The stronger the emotional response, the stronger the memory.

We may not remember the actual concrete facts of any particular event, but we do remember how the experience made us feel. We tend to then fill in the gaps within those memories based on the intense emotions we felt before, during, and after the event.

For example, let's say you gave a really bad speech in one of your college classes. You may not recall exactly what you said or did that made the speech as bad as you believed it was at the time, you just remember that you *felt* bad about it. You felt incredibly nervous before the speech, embarrassed during the speech, and ashamed afterward.

So now, when you drag that memory back up, while in reality you may have stuttered or lost your train of thought once or twice, your memory of it likely involves many more mistakes than actually occurred, or what other people, who

40

weren't as emotionally invested in the event, perceived to have occurred. Remember, we are all perceiving entirely different realities based on our focus.

Yet, while your memories of your past experiences are just fragmented illusions, they play a key role in shaping every single moment of your *present* reality. Your brain uses these past memories to assist in the interpretation of new stimuli, which means those past memories, whether real or imagined, have a key defining role in the construction of your current reality. History is constantly repeating itself. Or at least *your version* of it is.

As events unfold in the present, you interpret them based on past points of reference. This obscures the present moment and creates a skewed reality where everything happening in the now is being filtered through the past and ultimately, being dictated by it.

This is one of the reasons why so many marriages fail because you'd be hard-pressed to find a relationship that involves living together for so many years where there have not been disagreements and disappointments in the past. One word or phrase that the brain associates with one of those past events can set off the same argument that you've had for twenty years.

The phrase, "I have to work late tonight," can create a perception of reality for a new couple that their spouse is hard working, while the same phrase could create a perception of reality in which someone is cheating if there has been infidelity in the past. This is playing out every day in every single moment. A wet towel left on the floor, an incorrect food order, a forgotten anniversary – this could be viewed as a silly mistake, a simple and small infraction, or the last straw that ends a relationship.

The point is, the current moment is not just the current moment. It is always being filtered through the past and interpreted using the meaning we have given to past events. So how do you put a stop to this? How do you begin creating in the present moment rather than creating from the past?

Let's say that you again have to give a speech in front of an audience in the present day. Your thoughts immediately revert to your past experiences, and the meaning you have assigned to them, for answers on how to construct reality – how the future will play out.

The meaning that you may have assigned to that past experience was that you are bad at giving speeches and thus, your mind will become consumed with this idea. You will begin hoping that you don't do the same thing again, and assuming that you likely will since you are, after all, *bad at giving speeches*. You have assigned this proof based on your memory of the past.

You may even reinforce this thought out loud to everyone you come into contact with, telling them about your upcoming speech and why you are so nervous about it – because of how terrible the last speech you gave went. You may even find yourself exaggerating your re-telling of it to make for a better story, or simply because you don't actually remember all the details of it. Pretty soon, these exaggerations become your truth – you can't even remember that certain parts were exaggerated in the first place.

In the thinking of that bad speech, and in the hoping that you *don't* give another bad speech, by thinking about that possibility at all you are actually recreating the potential and drawing a similar event into your reality again. The more you think about it and recreate those events in your mind, the more likely it is to happen. It's like *practicing* for what you *don't* want to happen.

Imagine it like this, your past memories are all stored away in your mind like bags and bags of luggage that you have been choosing to carry along with you into the present everywhere you go. As an event occurs in the present, you sort through this luggage to pull meaning from these past memories. It's like pulling out clothes from the past and dressing the current moment in them to recreate that same perception over and over again.

But if you were to discard the baggage of the past, and there was no longer any load to carry, you would become weightless. Your potential would become limitless and your possibilities endless. You could then choose to dress the current moment in whatever outfit your imagination has the ability to create. This is why some people create alter-egos because the alter-ego has no past to pull from. They can be anyone they want to be, created moment to moment.

When you stop looking to the past for guidance on how the future will play out, the past stops projecting onto your future, opening up a world of new possibilities. By letting go of the past, you create freedom in the now, and in the now you can create an entirely new moment in time. And to do this you don't have to tell yourself to stop thinking about the past event (which will never work – remember that thinking about *not* thinking about it, is *still* thinking about it). Instead, you just have to build the new. You have to start thinking about a new event entirely.

Close your eyes and envision the timeline of your life as it likely appears to you now – a linear line where the past meets the present, which leads to the future. At the intersection of the past, and the future, where the present moment lies, erase the line before and after this present point in time. The dot that remains, out there on its own, with nothing but black space all around it is the juicy moment of now. It is the only place where you can find pure potential and true creative power. And it all starts right here, in your mind.

Imagine yourself standing on that dot indicating the present moment, with dark, empty space all around you. This moment is the beginning of your journey. Like a shining bright light in the darkness, this moment sheds light on an infinite number of entirely new timelines before you that are *anything but* linear.

These are your future possibilities, created only by your next thought, which creates your next step, in this very moment. What you choose to think now, what path you choose to step onto, creates an infinite number of new possibilities *in the now*. And in the now, *anything* is possible.

In the now, you have the ability to create an entirely new perception and assign new meaning to present events, rather than pulling meaning from the past. The present moment is a crystal clean slate. It's where you hold the most power and endless creative potential, where you can wave your magic wand, and mold the future into what you desire it to be. In the now, you can actually bend time, jump from one timeline to another, collapse timelines, or quantum leap into a new present reality. In the now, and only the now, you can create anything your heart desires.

Now is the time to create new memories. Instead of thinking about the past, and replaying it over and over again in your mind, erase that memory, and pivot your thoughts into creating a new memory from this current moment. Envision how you *want* the speech in the future to go. Visualize yourself at the podium *now*, in front of all of those people. Imagine yourself being calm, cool, and collected. Feel the feelings of being fully prepared and excited to share your knowledge with the room. Imagine the entire audience benefiting from your speech, enlightened with the new information you've shared with them. Imagine everything going perfectly and *feel* how you will feel when the speech is over and you have given the best speech of your life.

Keep doing this over and over again until the vision is so familiar to you, it is as if it were a memory, so vivid it is like it actually already happened. As Albert Einstein stated, "Imagination is your preview of life's coming attractions." Imagine how you want the coming attractions in your life to go, *not* how your memories of the past have gone. You can live out of your imagination rather than your memory. You can tie yourself to your limitless potential rather than your limiting past. You can create in the here and now, and it all starts within *you*.

There have been many studies done on mental practice and research has shown that visualization is often *even more effective* than physical practice. This is because your body cannot discern between an actual observed event happening in the now, versus a remembered event, or an imagined event.

Think about a fresh, juicy lemon. Now imagine yourself taking that lemon between your fingers and putting it to your mouth. Imagine taking a bite out of that lemon. What just happened inside your mouth? It responded to the lemon – it produced extra saliva, imagining the way the lemon tastes.

Studies have shown that the same neurons fire in your brain whether you are actually physically doing something, watching it happen, or simply imagining doing it. When you access a memory over and over again, it is like it is really happening over and over again. The same goes for visualizing – it is as if it is really happening each time that you visualize it.

Since it is easier to practice something in your mind perfectly a hundred times than it is to practice it in real life perfectly every single time, your mind truly is your most powerful tool. Even in the case of physical activities, such as playing a sport or an instrument, experiments show that you can be *more* effective just by sitting and visualizing doing it perfectly over and over again, than actually physically practicing the activity. Many of the best athletes in the world have admitted to doing this ritualistically before every game or match.

This is the work. It is not about actually doing the thing, it is about creating the experience in your mind and staying focused on it. That new experience, the new memory, the new expectation, will allow for the potentials and possibilities all around you to come alive. Do the work within and the outer experience will eventually follow.

When one repeatedly practices an activity or accesses a memory, the neurons in their brain create pathways that shape themselves according to that activity or memory. The more it is practiced or thought about, the stronger and thicker that neural pathway becomes. By visualizing how you want an event to go rather than accessing past memories of a similar event, you essentially disrupt the neural pathways in your brain and create new ones. You create new behaviors.

This, again, is called neural plasticity, and it is how you rewire your brain. Through repetition of the new activity or the new thought, those new neural pathways strengthen each time, overriding the old ones. This is not only how you master a new behavior, but how that new behavior eventually becomes habitual, something you don't even have to think about, something that just happens automatically for you and becomes your way of being. You simply become great at giving speeches.

Visualization also helps by taking your body out of panic mode when the event actually does occur. Without having visualized it ahead of time, the event is completely new to you, it is unfamiliar. The subconscious mind likes familiarity – remember, it is mostly concerned with your safety and survival first, and what is safer than the familiar? If you have been here before, if you have done this before, and you did not die, it must be safe.

It is not until your RAS has fulfilled its primary job of keeping you safe that it can move on and allow you to access the other areas of your brain responsible for intuition, rational, critical, and creative thinking. So rather than getting thrown into fight or flight mode when you step out on stage, and having your creative centers shut down, your nervous system is regulated, and you have better access to the parts of your brain responsible for innovation and thus, better performance.

Each time you use visualization rather than recalling a past memory you override your old programming. Your expectations change and you remove the unwanted possibility from your reality replacing it with the possibility of the new desired outcome. It really is that simple.

Erase the old memories that do not serve you by using visualization to create new ones. In your mind, you can do anything that you want to do and be anything that you want to be. You can be good at anything you want to be good at. Create a vivid experience in your mind of what you want and you will draw a similar potential to you. Add in watching other people perform perfect speeches and you will soon become unstoppable.

I envisioned myself in my dream home long before I moved into my dream home. I envisioned myself back at my ideal weight after each baby long before I reached my ideal weight. I envisioned myself working from home long before I was in a position to work from home. I envisioned myself quitting my job and writing full-time before I was anywhere close to being able to do that. I envisioned this book being written long before it was written. I envisioned people like you reading it long before this moment came to be.

I encourage you, too, to start daydreaming about the life you want. Imagine every detail, down to the way the silk sheets on the bed in your dream home feel upon waking in the morning and closing your eyes at night. Make it as real as possible in your mind and you will eventually make it your reality.

Think Bigger

As you chisel away at your thoughts ruthlessly discarding anything that does not serve you and making the space to think about what does, your focus will shift from problems and probabilities to solutions and possibilities. You will go from thinking about what is *likely* to happen, to asking yourself what *could be* possible. And the present moment will become a place of creation for you.
You'll find yourself asking, what do I *really* want? If I can really do, be, and have *anything* my heart desires, what would that look like?

As you dip your toes into the land of make-believe to pull ideas out of your fairytales into reality, you will start seeing the proof of what your focus is creating all around you. You will realize how powerful you truly are and will begin to wonder about the infinite potentials and possibilities available to you. You will begin to question the layers of limitations, constraints, and boundaries you once placed upon yourself.

And then, you will go bigger. This is the sweet spot. It is the reason you are here. The deepest desires in your heart are not random, they are specific to you, and they are there for a reason. There is something you are meant to do, something that *only you* can do. Something that no one else can do *quite* like you.

These desires may seem so big, so outlandish, so out of your reach, that you feel silly even admitting them to yourself. Before now, you may have disregarded these desires as impossible. But you will soon learn that *faith* in the impossible is what *creates* the possible.

> *"Create the highest, grandest vision possible for your life, because you become what you believe."*
>
> OPRAH WINFREY

FAITH

How your beliefs create reality.

PART II

Faith

\<noun\>

Strong or unshakeable belief in something, esp. without proof or evidence.

PART 2: FAITH

"And now these three remain: faith, hope, and love. But the greatest of these is love."

CORINTHIANS 13:13

OCTOBER 19, 2020

"Honey, I'm so sorry."

My husband stood in the doorway of our bedroom, the early morning sleep still in his eyes. He looked down at the phone in his hand where I noted a coffee *should* have been. I watched, curious, as he took a deep breath. Something that looked like agony ripped through his face as he fumbled to find the right words. And in that moment, I knew instantly that whatever came out of his mouth next would change everything.

I jolted upright into a sitting position in our bed and began to plead with God. *My parents*, I remember thinking. *No, no, no, no, no. Oh God, please, no. Not mom. Not dad. NO…*

"There was an accident at the lake house." A painstakingly long pause followed as Kyle shook his head in disbelief, mustering up the courage to finish.

Mom and Dad were at my sister's lake house this weekend? My mind raced as I tried to piece together and make sense of what I thought was coming. *Wait, an accident?*

"I'm so sorry, Kim…but Dana didn't make it."

My older sister. Dana Marie Bryant was 37 years old and had, what could only be described, as a picture-perfect life. She had a successful career, a beautiful home, a happy marriage, a stepson she loved dearly, and two of her own very young, happy, healthy, and adorable children. She had it all in a way that made most people, including me, completely envious of her. She was

49

gorgeous, incredibly charming, highly intelligent, and exceptionally talented. And she was so happy, so loved, *so full of life.*

And just like that, in the blink of an eye, she was gone.

Kyle shared with me the rest of the heartbreaking news. My sister's husband, my brother-in-law, Shawn, had been arrested. He was currently awaiting bail after spending the night in jail.

An ATV accident had taken the life of my sister, and Shawn had been the one driving. They had been sitting around a campfire at their lake house, with another couple after dark, when they had decided to take the ATV out to show their guests the huge reservoir being dug at the property next door. Their neighbor was building a man-made lake that was so incredibly big it was a sight to see. My sister's stepson, Cameron, then thirteen, had been left behind to watch over the children who had been put to bed earlier in the night.

As they were driving up a dirt hill around the lake's edge, the top-heavy vehicle hit some loose dirt and lost traction, causing it to turn sideways and topple down the steep hill. Of the four people in the ATV, Dana was the only one not wearing a seatbelt. Because of this, she fell out of the vehicle and it landed on top of her, instantly killing her with a blow to the head.

When police arrived on the scene, per protocol, the driver of the vehicle involved in the accident was given a breathalyzer. Shawn had only had a couple of beers, but while he was by no means drunk, he failed the DUI test. Due to this he had spent, what was no doubt, the worst night of his entire life in jail, and would soon be on trial for manslaughter.

On a typical Sunday morning, much like any other morning, I found myself thrown into an alternate reality where nothing was okay and nothing would ever be the same again. My sister was gone and my brother-in-law was in jail for murder. My precious five-year-old niece and seven-month-old nephew were without a mother *and* a father. My parents had lost their first-born child, their pride and joy, and mother to their grandchildren. And I had lost my big sister, my *only* sister – my keeper of secrets, my memory holder, my go-to advisor, my source of comfort and support, and life-long forever friend – the one person who knew and loved me in a way that no one else ever could.

These words, "Dana didn't make it," would become imprinted in my mind, destined to play on a never-ending loop – a constant reminder that life as I'd known it, was no more. Those four words had created a severance in time, a clearly marked *before* and *after,* where the vibrant colors of the before, filled with promise and hope and never-ending tomorrows, was swiftly replaced by the bleak grey of the after, an unforgiving and harsh reality of painful regrets and unfulfilled dreams.

In those first few moments after those four words were spoken, I remember how close the colorful before had remained, just within reach, so vivid, as if I could still reach out and grab it if I acted quickly enough, could still somehow stop it all from happening. My mind wrestled with this idea chaotically, relentless in its pursuit of trying to keep our world from plummeting into darkness. I grasped at the before, clawed at it, desperately tried to hold on to it. But with each passing second, the darkness closed in around me. I watched, defeated, as the colorful before drifted slowly away, further and further out of reach, until it was gone forever. Until all that was left around me was the bleak, grey, nothingness of the after.

The perfectly straight timeline of our lives, as I'd once imagined it, took a sharp drastic turn, as though we'd missed the train to our predictably perfect future and had been forced to hop onto another timeline entirely. This new timeline was one that was unfamiliar and impossible to navigate – one that had no rule book or obvious path to follow. We were in uncharted territory, with no idea where we were headed, what sharp turns might be up ahead, or how long and treacherous the journey might be.

And at the root of it all, this timeline was missing the one single person who would know exactly what to do. The one person who would have typically taken control of the situation and handled everything with grace and efficiency. The one person who I could always lean on to guide me through the unknown, the uncomfortable, and the downright hard things in life.

In the coming days and weeks, I would take on the role of my big sister. I would talk to the coroner, to science donation programs, to human resources at her work, and to her insurance companies. I would talk to the local newspaper and write her obituary. I would talk to a pastor and a funeral director and plan out her service. I would talk to her friends about speaking at her funeral and write a speech of my own. I would research and talk to many child and family psychologists to set up appointments for Shawn and the kids. I would even talk to a district attorney, along with my parents, to plead for the manslaughter case against my brother-in-law to be dropped.

All of these conversations with strangers, and yet I would have no idea what to say to the ones I loved. The ones hurting beyond anything anyone could ever imagine. Words simply were not enough.

"I'm so sorry this happened to you." My first words, *my true feelings*, upon embracing my brother-in-law, who'd been released on bail in the early afternoon following the accident. I couldn't fathom the torture he'd been through, and was still going through. He was understandably disheveled and still visibly shaking. His face, a pale white, contrasted by the extremely dark circles under his eyes. I walked in to find him pacing back and forth in his kitchen, staring at his hands out in front of him, as if they weren't his own, mumbling to himself like you might see someone doing in an insane asylum.

"I know you're worried about your dad. He's going to be okay; I promise." My first words, *a lie*, to my sister's 13-year-old stepson. I had *no idea* if his father was going to be okay. Cameron had been inside the lake house that night, keeping an eye on the sleeping children. He was the one to call his mother after the accident, who would then be the one to call my parents. He would later share that he didn't think he would ever be able to get his dad's tortured screams that night out of his head. From inside the lake house, he'd heard them coming from quite a distance away. *Some kind of wild animal has been hurt*, he'd thought at first.

"This just can't be real." My words to my mother upon seeing her and my father's devastated and tired faces. They both looked as though they had aged ten years overnight. They had rushed to the lake house in the middle of the night after receiving the worst phone call a parent could ever receive. There, they'd waited hours for the sun to come up, for their grandchildren to wake up, and for their son-in-law to be released on bail, before joining him to break the devastating news to my niece and nephew.

Kylie, then five, and Caleb, seven months, had gone to bed the night before in a world where all was right, tucked in by their mommy, only to wake up in this upside-down, parallel universe, where she was gone.

I picked up my baby nephew and hugged him tightly. He was the only one who had no need for words. He looked confused, picking up on the emotions in the room, yet unable to comprehend them. I remember the way his eyes constantly scanned the room around him, as if looking for her everywhere. For months to come, every time he cried, we'd imagined it was for her.

"I love you so much. Everything is going to be okay." My anguished words to my five-year-old niece. Once again, *a lie*. Nothing was going to be okay. Of this, I was certain. Kylie, at five years old, simply could not understand where heaven was, or why her mother had gone there – why she was now *there*, instead of *here*, or what *forever* actually meant. It was both a curse and a blessing that she didn't understand. I'm not sure that any of us could have taken it if she was able to fully comprehend, if she was able to fully feel the crushing weight of what had happened, as we all were.

But with my promise to my niece came a great responsibility that we leaned into. I would do everything I could to try to make it all okay. I would take Dana's place as best as I possibly could. In the coming days, my husband and I, and our two-year-old son, would pack up our lives and move in with my brother-in-law. He needed support, my niece and nephew needed a mother, and ultimately, we needed to put into place what could inevitably end up being necessary if a grand jury decided to rip their dad out of their lives forever, just as their mother had been.

The truth was, regardless of the outcome from the trial, we had no idea how Shawn would cope. While he was one of the most level-headed, capable human beings I had ever met, it would have been understandable if he had decided that he could no longer deal with the hand he'd been dealt. No one would have blamed him if the sleepless nights and the nightmares, and the guilt, and the shame, and the fear of what was to come, as well as the outright heartbreak, broke him.

But Shawn didn't break. He held together the pieces of what was left with all that he had. Putting one foot in front of the other, he focused on what he *could* control, while attempting to do the impossible – to fill the deep, dark hole of their mother's loss that was felt in every corner of their home, again, with love and joy. To recreate the magical childhood for his kids that Dana had been such a huge part of.

He knew this would not be possible if he didn't take care of himself first. So, he took the necessary steps that he needed to for his kids. He went to see his doctor and was prescribed sleeping pills and an antidepressant. He attended counseling and read books on coping with grief. Upon being terminated due to the negative publicity, from his very successful career as an insurance agent, that he'd spent his entire life building, he started over with a brand-new career. He invested in and became a partner in his best friend's construction business. This was a choice that would allow him more freedom in his schedule so that he could show up for his kids as a single parent.

From day one, Shawn never relied on me to mother his children. He became father *and mother* to his children himself. He got out of bed every morning, forced a smile on his face, and took care of them, his standard response becoming, "Thanks, but I got this." He excused himself to a dark room to cry when needed, always away from the kids, and somehow found a way in the midst of all of his sadness to make a happy home again, to bring joy and laughter back into their lives, and to go above and beyond what anyone could have ever expected of him. He told us that he could never fill Dana's shoes because she wasn't just a mother, she was an *incredible* mother. But for her, he would do everything he could to be the best dad that he could be. He would do everything he could to make her proud of him.

It was only a couple months after we'd moved in that we decided Shawn was going to be okay and that he could handle being on his own. We felt it was time to give him the space he needed to put his life back together. Us being there felt unsettled, as though it was keeping everyone suspended in the void of the after. He agreed that he was ready and we moved back into our home with a plan in place to spend as much time with him and the kids as possible.

But Shawn's sanity and the kid's happiness was only one of the battles that needed to be overcome. The Covid-19 pandemic kept pushing his trial date later and later. Although Shawn's team of lawyers were optimistic in the way that they spoke with us at first, as we got closer to the trial, they began preparing us more for what was to come. They made it clear that Shawn would not likely get off the hook for what had happened. After all, Shawn had a DUI record from his not-so-distant youth, two boating incidents and a public intoxication charge, all prior to meeting Dana. This would no doubt be used in the state's evidence against him.

It was not until after my parents and I had driven an hour to see the district attorney to plead for the charges against Shawn to be dropped, that we were made aware of this information. We had spent a considerable amount of time defending Shawn's character, describing him as a law-abiding citizen with a spotless record. We'd pleaded with the D.A. to take into consideration that he was in his backyard when this freak accident occurred, not out on the road endangering others. The district attorney had agreed to look into the case and get back to us.

It was as we were placing pictures of Dana around the funeral home – pictures of her with her babies, pictures of her holding her pregnant belly, pictures of her in her white dress on her wedding day, in her college and high school graduation caps, and in pigtails and bows as a little girl herself – and still grappling with coming to terms that this was all real, that *she was really gone* – when my dad got the call. The district attorney asking us if we knew about Shawn's record.

His *what*? I'll never forget the feeling that day as my stomach dropped to the floor, the wind taken out of our sails so swiftly. What little bit of hope we'd held on to that we would be able to regain some kind of normalcy was gone. *All was lost.*

Shawn would go to court. He would sit in front of a grand jury who would hear all about his past. This time *someone had been killed.* Shawn would be convicted of manslaughter. There was no doubt in my mind.

I could feel the walls of that funeral home closing in around me as I imagined my dearly beloved brother-in-law in that tiny cell, separated from his children who would grow up without him there, the love of his life gone, his family ripped apart, and nothing in front of him but those four walls for years to come. For an accident that truly was not his fault, for something that he would blame himself for, for the rest of his life, anyway.

This could not be real. This was the stuff you saw in movies, not something that happened to *us*. Not something that happened to *my* family.

As the trial loomed, Shawn's lawyers prepared him as best they could. They let him know that his record would, indeed, play a huge role in the outcome. While the sentencing could go multiple ways, they were quite sure he would be convicted. We got more and more sick to our stomachs with each passing day as we waited in hopeless anticipation.

Shawn, on the other hand, went to work. He didn't wait for the outcome of the trial. He never spoke of what was likely to happen, never allowed himself to believe that he was going to prison, and continued to act as though he were not. He invested in his future, continued to build the company he'd become a partner in, and made future plans for himself and his kids, as though prison was not even a potential reality for him. And so, we followed his lead, and plans were never made in the event that the worst came to be. We would cross that bridge when it came.

In the midst of all of this chaos, pain, and heartbreak, I realized something very important, something that would change everything for me. I realized that I had not only taken my sister for granted my entire life, but that I had been taking my *own* life for granted too.

I had been sleeping my way through life, wishing away my days, and putting my dreams on the backburner as if there were an infinite number of tomorrows. As if there would always be plenty of time later to do all the things I wanted to do in this lifetime. But the veil had been lifted and now I saw how quickly everything could change and how truly limited our time here really was. I could be gone tomorrow too, swiftly removed from this world as quickly as my sister had been.

I realized that I had been living my life in fear, too scared to step off the well-beaten path. Fear of what people thought of me, fear of failure, of rejection, of letting others down – these fears had me living a life that was not of my choosing, but rather, one of conformity. I had spent my life striving for a safe, mediocre existence. But where had that fear gotten me? It certainly didn't stop the worst from happening. One day, I would die too. And when I did, would I be proud of the legacy I'd left behind? Would I be proud of the example my life would leave for my son? Would I be proud of what I had accomplished, of all of the hours I had spent working on someone else's dreams, rather than pursuing my own?

My dream since I had been a little girl had always been to become a best-selling author. I'd always imagined a life of passion and purpose, one of total freedom, doing what I loved to do. In these daydreams, my life would be spent by the pool, or on a beach, or in a cafe, feverishly writing away, off in another world of my own creation. My books would not only entertain, but inspire, and educate my readers, and make a real difference in their lives, much like some of my favorite authors had made in mine. I would leave behind a legacy, my own mark on the world in ink, never to be forgotten.

Now I wondered when exactly had I let fear take over? When did I "grow up" and decide work was more important than my dreams? When did I decide that I was going to spend the majority of my life doing something so insignificant to me, rather than working toward those dreams? When did I decide to put my faith in some entity that could care less about me, rather than putting faith in myself, in the dreams written on my heart, in the vision I held within for my life?

As I watched the lives of everyone that I loved crumbling all around me, I realized that if Shawn could have faith in the face of everything he had been dealt, then I could too. I decided it was time to transmute my fear into something far more powerful – to alchemize my fear into faith. Because at the end of the day, at the end of my life, it was a far scarier potential to look back and realize that I'd never really lived at all. That I hadn't even *tried* to live the life I'd always dreamed of.

I made the decision that I was going to really go after my dreams, not in the small-scale way that I had been up to this point, fitting in writing when I had the chance, daydreaming about it, but not really believing in it. But rather, in an all-in, massive way. I would make it my number one priority and put all of my energy into creating the life I'd always dreamed of. I wouldn't let anything stand in my way – certainly not a job that I didn't even really like that much.

And if I failed, then so be it, but I couldn't accept not trying. This, I decided, would be the silver lining in the wake of my sister's death. I made a promise to myself to live, *truly* live my life, and pursue my dreams, in the way I knew that she would want me to. In the same way that she'd always pursued hers.

It took me four years, more work than I could have ever imagined, and many tears, to write this book. But in those four years, I never lost faith. Every time I faltered, had to take a break to regain my sanity, questioned my commitment, abilities, or talent, and wanted to quit, I reminded myself of that promise. I reminded myself of my *why*. And I reminded myself that anything is possible, as long as you *believe* it is. I saw this first hand as I watched Shawn, too, see the power of his faith come to fruition.

More than a year after the accident, Shawn finally went to court. My father testified on his behalf. He told the jury that he wanted, *more than anyone*, to have someone to blame for this accident. He had lost his daughter and he desperately wanted to hate someone for it. But he had seen the proof for himself that there was no one to blame.

When my dad arrived at the lake house in the middle of the night, he walked to the scene of the accident, because he had to see for himself what had happened. He'd followed the tracks up the hill and saw where the ATV hit the mound of loose dirt at the top. He saw where it lost traction, got turned sideways, and ended up toppling down the hill.

He saw for himself that this was an accident that had nothing to do with alcohol or careless driving. As a matter of fact, if Shawn had been going just a little faster, rather than taking the hill so slowly, the ATV may not have lost traction like it had. It wasn't a joy ride that turned bad, but a freak accident that could have never been anticipated.

And while my dad would never be able to get that scene out of his mind, as it would play on repeat every single time he closed his eyes at night, and upon waking in the morning, he was glad he did it. He was glad that he'd had the wherewithal to take pictures of the tire markings in the dirt, which were washed away the very next day by rain. Those pictures served as proof in Shawn's defense that the accident was *in fact an accident*, out of his control.

My father pleaded with the jury to see that Shawn had been punished enough and that there was nothing they could do to him that would be worse than what had already happened. He showed the jury pictures of my niece and nephew and told them that *they* would be the ones most punished if their father was taken away too. He begged them to believe him when he said that Shawn was the best father to these children, better than anyone could ever imagine. And that it would be *their lives* most affected if they grew up without a mother *and* without a father.

And then, in what Shawn's team of lawyers would describe only as a miracle, the jury decided to drop all felony charges against him, charging him only with a misdemeanor, which too, was later dismissed. Shawn was free. He wouldn't be taken away from his children and we could all breathe again.

And I couldn't help but think, it was Shawn's unyielding faith in the *impossible* that had made it all *become possible*.

> *"All it takes is faith and trust…and just a little bit of pixie dust."*
>
> PETER PAN

Shawn, Dana, Kylie, Caleb, and Cameron

LESSONS ON FAITH

"Therefore, I tell you, whatever you ask for in prayer,
believe that you have received it, and it will be yours."

MARK 11:24

A Higher Power

Throughout your life you will inevitably hear this word, *Faith*.

There will likely come a time when you will be encouraged, or even expected, to succumb to some type of indoctrination into a particular faith. This may come from both strangers and people you know – perhaps even people you trust, admire, or want to make proud.

You may also hear messages to the contrary of this, such that the concept of faith, especially faith in God, is in strict opposition to science. Many would argue that you cannot believe in both, that you have to choose one or the other – God *or* science. Some may even go as far as to call organized religion a conspiracy or a cult. It certainly could be argued that religious belief can be found at the root cause of so many wars and countless other evils throughout history. An image of the first Christian missionaries wielding a cross in one hand, and a sword in the other, comes to mind.

Rest assured, while I am a believer of Science, I am not here to tell you *not* to believe in God, because *I* believe in God. However, in a world in which religion is often taught right alongside math, science, and geography as if it is no different, in which the loudest arguments are often from the farthest reaches of the spectrum, drowning out anyone in the middle, and in which people tend to present their beliefs as fact, rather than opinion, what I *am* here to do, is to remind you that no matter how convincing one might be, *no one knows anything for sure.*

Beware of anyone that tells you that they do. Beware of anyone that positions themselves as an authority on God or places themselves as an intermediary *between* you and God (or whatever word your faith uses in reference to this higher power). Beware of anyone who makes you feel inferior because your beliefs do not align with their own, or makes you feel as though you are doing something wrong by questioning God, religion, or spiritual practices.

And while we're at it, beware of anyone who uses fear tactics to gain your allegiance, cherry-picks words from a 2,700-year-old book to prove their ideas (while blatantly ignoring others), and/or leads you to believe that there is something intrinsically wrong with you that only they, or someone else, can fix.

Let's get this out of the way right now. You, my darling, are not a sinner that needs to be saved. You are not a bad little boy or a bad little girl, nor should you ever worry about being something as subjective as "good" in the first place. You are *you* and that, alone, is all you ever need to be. Your existence is a miracle and you are perfect just as you are, just as perfect as you were the day that you were born into this world. You are worthy simply because you are. Because we *all* are. *Worthy of what?* You might ask. *Everything.* You *are* everything and you *deserve* everything that this world has to offer, just as much as anyone else does. Don't you dare listen to anyone who tells you that you do not.

Anyone or anything that assumes the superiority of one group over another is something that should be avoided at all costs. This is not intended to serve as anti-religion speak, but rather as *historical perspective*. The division of people based on some belief of the inherent worthiness of one group over another is what has led to such atrocities as world wars, human slavery, and mass genocides. No group is superior to another, regardless of race, nationality, *or* religion. It is a scary thing when a group or an individual, even one that *means* no harm, declares their superiority over another. This is especially concerning when it is done, as is so often the case, around naïve and unsuspecting ears, placing an unnecessary and dangerous divide among the next generation.

Even if religious believers did use caveats such as "I believe…" or "Some believe…", rather than stating their opinions as fact, it wouldn't matter. In psychology, it's called the "mere exposure effect" or the "repetition effect". In marketing, it's called the "familiarity principle." Whatever you hear over and over and over again, you develop a likeness for, you develop a trust in, *you believe*. Your beliefs are, after all, simply thoughts that you keep thinking, which typically come from that which you have heard over and over again. This is why most people *are* what *their people are* – whether that be Jewish, or Muslim, or Christian, or so on. Repetition builds credibility.

It is also the reason why so many drink the proverbial Kool-Aid. It's not our fault. It's simply how our minds are designed to work. It's how humans learn. If we hear it over and over and over again, our brains recognize that it must be important. It *must* be true. The brain begins seeking out the proof of that belief.

And in a world of infinite possibilities, there is *always* proof to be found for *every* belief.

This is unfortunately the reason why planes were flown into the World Trade Center and bombs set off at the Boston Marathon; why sacrificial rituals are performed, why women are stoned to death in some countries for showing their hair, why journalists are beheaded, and why abortion clinics are blown up. It's why countless wars have been started and millions of people tortured and murdered throughout history. Because a child, or a teenager, or an adult, and often at each one of these stages, was told the same message over and over again. And so, whatever the message, it became their truth.

I don't have any truths for you here about a white-haired man in the sky known for keeping a naughty and nice list, as depicted by many of the major world religions. I will simply say that I stopped believing in Santa Claus a long time ago. I do not expect, nor desire, for you to believe in what I believe in, and so I will not share with you all of my presumably flawed thoughts and opinions on God. But what I do desire is to share with you a different perspective on faith in the hope that it may open your mind to a new world of possibility.

I believe it is far more important to know *how* to think than knowing *what* to think, and that is especially true when it comes to your spirituality and the meaning that you give to life. As the scientist, Carl Sagan, declared, "Who is more humble? The scientist who looks at the Universe with an open mind and accepts whatever the Universe has to teach us, or somebody who says everything in this book must be considered the literal truth and never mind the fallibility of all the human beings involved?"

Of course, this book he is referring to is the bible. Both atheists and theists point to this book to argue for or against their faith, but this book does not prove or disprove a single thing. The bible is a man-made book, the stories handed down by word of mouth over the span of hundreds of thousands of years. These stories were written by many different authors, in many different places, and for many different people, due to many different agendas. The stories have been translated, revised, reinterpreted, altered, added to, and had countless others removed. Regardless of what anyone tells you, by design, it simply cannot be taken word for word as the ultimate truth. I say this not with a lack of faith, but with the smallest inkling of intelligence.

Nevertheless, the bible is a great piece of literature, and as is the case with all great literature, there is certainly *some* truth that can be found within its pages. For this reason, I do not knock anyone who uses it as a source of inspiration so long as they are doing so with a discerning eye. There are plenty of quotes I personally love from the bible and you will see that I have used many of them in this section. This has been done intentionally as an attempt to bridge the gap between religion and science as I believe there to be many commonalities. But please understand, it is in no way a declaration that the bible is the end-all-be-all for my faith, and I would never wish for it to serve as that for yours either.

If there is one piece of advice that I can give you as it relates to *all* things, not just religious or spiritual faith, it is this: Blind faith in someone else's words is not an attribute to be sought after. As Albert Einstein said, "Blind belief in authority is the greatest enemy of truth."

For that in which there is no proof, it is in your best interest to question. You should not only question, but hypothesize, research, and experiment to *find* truth. This is the scientific method and it is how we determine fact from fiction.

But I would like to take that a step further and say that even for that in which there *is* proof, it is *still* in your best interest to question. For what is true in one experiment, time, place, mind, or life, may not be true in another. There are *always* variables at play, sometimes *unknown* variables that can be very difficult to identify. It is for this reason that you should be of the mindset to question *everything*, especially deeply rooted ideas about that which has always been as these simply do not get questioned enough.

The biggest variable at play when asking the question, *is God real?* is the definition of God, itself. If you asked 100 people what God means to them, you would likely get 100 different answers. For this one variable alone, it is imperative that you take what anyone else has to say about God with a grain of salt because you could simply be talking about two very different things. This has been my experience time and time again, as my definition of God does not typically align with others.

Contrary to popular belief, I don't adhere to the notion of a higher power that must be feared, one that is wrathful and judgmental. I don't believe in a God that both loves us unconditionally and in the same vein, is ready and willing to use his staff to exile us to hell for our sins for all of eternity. As a matter of fact, I don't believe this higher power to be an individual in any sense of the word, with man-like tendencies and opinions, choosing to answer some prayers and not others, playing favorites over his own creations. And I certainly don't believe that "he" cares one bit what you call "him".

I think using pronouns such as "he" and "him" to describe this higher power to only be a misrepresentation of what it actually is, and a trivial one at that. But if you want to give God eyes, ears, a nose, and a mouth, *not to mention a race and a gender*, in order to conceptualize the source of everything, then by all means, carry on. I am not here to tell you what to believe, I just want you to understand that there are many different definitions for God other than the one you have most likely heard the loudest throughout your entire life.

What I'd like to offer you here is not a rigid definition of God, but a flexible one – a God that you need not lack understanding of and fear, but rather one that you can understand and love. I believe that this is what we are all inherently searching for, after all – a God that is fair and just, and a divine order that is as close to perfection as one can humanly conceptualize.

The truth is, it doesn't matter what anyone else thinks. You must find your *own* meaning for God, for life, for the Universe, for miracles, for Source, Spirit, the Divine, or whatever other word resonates with you.

The name one gives their faith, or the word one uses to describe it, is not important. What *is* important and what I'd like you to consider (not trust or believe, but rather hypothesize) is that there *is a higher power* and that it is *everywhere*, and in *everything*. This almighty power resides within *you*, just as it does within *all* beings and *all* things. And most importantly, I'd like you to consider the idea that through this higher power, absolutely *all things are possible*.

The Impossible

"And Jesus said unto him, 'If thou canst believe, all things are possible to him that believeth.'" Mark 9:23.

In 1954, Roger Bannister broke the world record by running a mile in under four minutes. Prior to this feat, the best athletes in the world had tried and failed for almost a decade to beat the last world record held at four minutes and 1.3 seconds. During this time, it was deemed by the public, by scientists, and athletes alike, to be physically impossible to run a four-minute mile.

Bannister, however, decided that not only could the impossible be done, but that he would be the one to do it. This decision changed history.

When he stepped on to that starting line on May 6, 1954, he did so with a confidence the world had never seen. Bannister had spent months before the race engrossed in his practice, studying the mechanics of running and developing and trying out new methods.

Even though all current, physical evidence pointed to it being *impossible*, he held on firmly to his belief in what *was possible*. When the conditions that day turned out to be less than favorable, he gave absolutely no attention to the rain-soaked path and extreme winds that could keep his dreams from being realized. When he found himself both behind on time, as well as behind other runners at the halfway mark, he didn't lose faith. Nothing was going to stop him from doing what he believed could be done.

And because of that, he became a legend.

Another legend from my hometown, Muhammad Ali, told the entire world he was the greatest boxer of all time *before* he actually was. There were plenty of critics at the time that construed his claims as arrogance, at best, and complete disillusion, at worst. But those opinions meant nothing to him because those opinions were not *his* truth.

Ali had an unyielding faith, a belief in himself so fierce, so powerful, that it melted away all limitations and doubts from his mind. Despite obstacle after obstacle, including being stripped of his heavyweight title and being banned from boxing for 3 1/2 years during the prime of his career, Muhammad Ali's truth would prevail. He would not only be named the greatest boxer of all time, but he would hold that title to this day, some 60 years later, even after his death.

Ali once stated, "Impossible is just a big word thrown around by small men who find it easier to live in the world they've been given than to explore the power they have to change it. Impossible is not a fact. It's an opinion.

Impossible is not a declaration. It's a dare. Impossible is potential. Impossible is temporary. Impossible is nothing."

Legends, like Roger Bannister and Muhammad Ali, hold a vision of themselves as the legend they are striving to become long before there is any physical evidence of it being possible. Because of this, they are often doubted, criticized, and even ridiculed for their belief in themselves. But rather than letting other people's opinions sway their own, rather than staying within the box already created for them, they are steadfast and unapologetic in the face of all doubt. With every naysayer, that belief only grows stronger. With every obstacle and every failure, they become more committed to their vision.

This is faith. It is when you believe beyond all reasonable doubt, *not* based on what *someone else* has said or done, but based on the vision within you, the vision that only you can see, the vision that you believe deep down to your core is meant to be, even when the physical proof has yet to appear. Even when the current physical proof may say that it is not possible. Even when it looks like it cannot possibly happen, or even actually *fails* to happen, again and again. In a world of infinite possibilities, faith alone keeps possibility alive.

Creating Miracles

"Ask, and it shall be given you; seek, and ye shall find; knock, and it shall be open unto you." – Matthew 7:7.

So much of what you see in the world around you was at one time considered a miracle. What was once deemed impossible becomes a reality every single day by people who refuse to lose faith. Take a moment to marvel at the miracles around every corner, things that were at one time, no doubt, considered impossible.

We lived in caves and now we live in temperature-controlled houses with electricity, refrigeration, and plumbing.

We caught or killed our food and dressed it ourselves and now we go to the supermarket, or restaurants, and have groceries, or prepared foods, delivered right to our doorstep.

We travelled by foot and then used horse drawn carriages and sailboats, and now we have automobiles, engine-powered boats, air, and even space travel.

We wrote letters to one another that would arrive weeks or months later by foot and now we type a message on a computer or a cell phone that instantly arrives in front of another person, even if they are thousands of miles away.

We painted on cave walls, and then we had books and encyclopedias and libraries, and now we have the internet and search engines, video tutorials, AI, audiobooks and podcasts on all subjects available to us at all times, at the simple press of a button.

We had very little to no protection, treatments, or cures for viruses and diseases and now we have vaccinations, antibiotics, and life-enhancing and life-saving drugs and surgeries available to us. Today, scientists are working on 3D printed organs, stem cell injections that literally turn back the biological age, and nanobots injected into people to perform surgeries.

Nothing is impossible. Yet, all of these things were certainly considered impossible before they were accomplished, invented, or created. The idea of these were so outside of the realm of thinking before their time that they likely were not even considered at all by anyone but that one person who had that one genius idea within them.

As Steve Jobs once famously said, "The people who are crazy enough to think they can change the world are the ones who do." If you would have tried to explain a microwave to someone in 1944, just a year before it was invented, or the internet to someone in 1992, right before it was introduced to the public, the people in that time period would have thought you were crazy.

Yet somewhere, some *crazy* person had a *crazy* idea. They had a vision that no one else could see. And they saw that vision so clearly and believed in it so strongly, they were able to convince others of its efficacy, and bring it to life. They put that vision at the forefront of their minds and lives, pushed past their fear of what other people might think of them, pushed past the inevitable failure after failure that comes with the creation of something new, and eventually, created a miracle.

"Do not conform to the pattern of this world, but be transformed by the renewing of your mind." Romans 12:2. Roger Bannister refused to conform to popular belief. What began as a thought that he kept thinking, turned into a belief, and then became a reality. It took ten years of attempts and failures and people saying it couldn't be done before he did the impossible. But after he did, it was no longer deemed impossible. Once he broke through that glass ceiling of impossibility, it gave permission for others to do the same.

As other runners saw the proof that it could be done, they started believing they could do it too, and the four-minute mile quickly became routine. Nothing about anyone's ability changed, they had the ability all along, but their limiting beliefs kept them from reaching for it. It was both the faith that it *couldn't* be done that had *stopped* runners from achieving it, and the faith that it *could* be done that had *allowed* them to achieve it.

This is a phenomenon often referred to as the "psychological barrier" or the "barrier effect." It occurs when people believe that a certain achievement, such as breaking a track record in this case, is impossible. Once one person successfully accomplishes it, it can shift the perception of what's achievable, inspiring others to attempt and achieve the same feat, or *sometimes even greater ones* as their minds open to new potentials and they build upon that first possibility.

While it took my son, Knox, a little over a year to learn to walk, and much convincing to even try, my second born, Khloe, took her first steps at eight months and was full blown walking by ten months. She saw her brother, someone similar in size to herself, walking around on two legs and therefore, believed it was possible for her to do the same.

She was relentless in her pursuit. She wobbled on those little legs, unsteady as a baby deer, as they gave out on her time and time again. She tripped and face planted more times than I could count, making me a nervous wreck, and making *her* all the more determined.

Oh, how I'd wished that she would wait a little longer to try to walk. She was just so tiny, and weak, and uncoordinated. She didn't even have the ability to put out her hands to break her fall. This is a typical response from those that love us and want to keep us safe when we attempt to step out into the unknown. But Khloe would have nothing to do with *my* fears. She would push my hands away and although she couldn't yet talk, her stern look spoke for itself. "Don't you *dare* try to stop me. I'm going to do this." Her resolve was unwavering.

And then, she did it. She took her first steps, and we rejoiced, and she did it again, and again, and again, until she was so good at it, she began to run.

At only eight months old, Khloe innately understood how it all worked. She understood that if someone else could do it, that only meant that she could do it too. She understood that each time she failed she was gaining a critical piece of information that was essential to her success. That every time she got back up to try again, she was not just *starting from scratch*, but *starting from experience* – each failure taking her one step closer to her goal. She would not give up, there was no question in her mind about that, and so, she knew she *would* eventually succeed.

Perhaps this faith in herself was easier for Khloe than it had been for her brother, Knox, because she had the proof of what was possible right in front of her eyes, taunting her with its possibility every day. This is surely why the second child always seems to do things so much quicker than the first. The proof that the idea is possible is already there, it just takes believing in themselves that *they* can do it too.

But how does one get back up and try again, or try at all in the first place, when there is no proof that something can be done? How does one convince themselves that they're not just wasting their time or making a fool of themselves? How do they convince themselves to believe that something *can* be done when it doesn't seem possible, has never been attempted, or has only been failed at before?

Faith. As Corinthians 5:7 states, "For we walk by faith, not by sight." Before anything was done for the first time, including the first human being to walk on two legs, there was but only faith. A belief, beyond all reasonable doubt, that *anything* is possible. And not just possible, but possible for *you*.

You are the Creator

A Harvard University study, known as the Hotel Maid Study, performed an experiment to study the effect of brain priming on the staff of seven different hotels.

Half of the participants were informed about how much exercise they were getting every day through their work – how many calories they burned, how similar vacuuming is to a work out, etc. The other half were given no such information.

Several weeks later, it was found that the first group who had been primed to think of their work as exercise, had actually lost weight. Incredibly, these individuals had not done any more work or exercised any more than the control group – their colleagues who had *not* been informed about how their work was similar to a workout.

This is the power of belief in action. It can reshape both mind *and* physical reality. It can literally reshape the human body. As St. Augustine put it, "Faith is to believe in what you do not see. The reward of this faith is to see what you believe." In other words, you must believe it to see it.

There have been many experiments on the mind's role in the perception of reality. A great example of this is the placebo effect, which has been studied at great length. During these experiments, sugar pills were given to patients with extreme pain symptoms, while informing them that the pill would reduce or cure their pain, even though it contained no such ingredients to do so. Each time, the patients, believing the pill would help them, experienced a miraculous curing of pain.

People in wheelchairs have stood up and walked again after being blessed by religious leaders. Pagans of the past used to pray to multiple gods to help them win battles or to find meat to feed their families. Native Americans used song and dance to bring on the rain.

Sugar pills, blessings, multiple gods, spirits – it's all *just* belief. And belief is powerful. It can alter both mind and reality. But these are all examples of, what I like to call, *diluted* belief – belief that is pointed outward rather than inward. Belief that requires a run-through entity, something outside of oneself, that is given the credit for one's own good fortune or success, or perhaps lack thereof. Yet, the common denominator is always the same – the person's internal belief – *their faith* – in a possibility.

While each of these examples could be perceived as miracles, there have certainly been far greater miracles that have occurred. People have spontaneously cured themselves of disease using modalities such as meditation, spiritual healing, and other holistic remedies. Mothers have acquired super human strength in the face of impossible situations to save their children, such as lifting 4,000-pound cars off of babies. Doctors have brought people back to life past the point of no return – there is even one case of a doctor saving a child after more than an hour of resuscitation.

And while all of these could be perceived as miracles that only the power of God could perform, I encourage you to pull back the veil and discover the hidden truth within.

The person dying of cancer very well may have prayed to God to find a cure, but they found and implemented that cure *themselves*.

Upon witnessing a car roll on top of her baby, the mother may have prayed to God in that moment to save her child, but she didn't sit back and wait for God to lift the car – she lifted the car *herself*.

The doctor resuscitating the child may have prayed for God's help while he worked, but he didn't sit back and wait for God to save his patient – he did that *himself*, with his own two hands.

They all may have prayed to God, or Allah, or Shiva, or Jehovah, or their spirits, or angels for help. *Or, not*. Regardless of their religious or spiritual beliefs, or lack thereof, each miracle started with a single person's faith in themselves. Faith in their own abilities created the will *and* the way. And without that unshakeable faith, even if held just for a single, precious moment in time, the inspired actions that led to these miracles could have never occurred. That intense, unwavering belief in themselves allowed them to tap into a powerful source within. And that powerful energy flowed directly through their fingertips, *creating* the miracle.

I once heard a debate between a theist and an atheist that has always stuck with me. The religious man, Dr. John Lennox, said, "The idea that God and science are competing explanations is a failure to understand the nature of explanation itself." He said that "God no more competes with science as an explanation of the Universe than Henry Ford competes with automobile engineering as an explanation for the motor car. You need both. Just as you admire Henry Ford's genius when you see the motorcar, so you can admire God's genius (when you see the inner workings of the Universe)."

He went on to ask the atheist to consider the question, "why does water boil?" The scientific explanation could be that the thermal energy from the fire is transferred to the water causing the water molecules to gain energy and move faster. However, you could also use an agent explanation, and say that the water is boiling because *I want a cup of tea*. Both are simultaneously true and it is both that gives you a full explanation.

While the religious man was most definitely *not* trying to make the point that the "I" wanting a cup of tea was God, if you look closely at what he's said, does it not stand to argue that you, and I, and Henry Ford are the creators, as it is our desires, and the energetic force within us, that begins the process of all creation?

Science, even science that we do not yet understand, which is what we often refer to as miracles, is simply the magic one uses to create. We do not always understand this magic, just like cavemen did not understand the chemical reaction that is fire when they found a way to cook their food and keep themselves warm. But that is what makes it all the more incredible – that this "magic" is here for us to call upon, even when we do not yet understand how or why, and can come together for us by sheer faith and will alone. It is *divine* creation.

"Yes, he was fully man, but he was also fully God." – Colossians 2:9. Just as Jesus was believed to have not only been the son of God (John 3:16), but also to be God himself – God in human flesh (1 Timothy 3:16), are we not also believed to be God's children, as well as created in God's image? Can we not, too, turn water into wine, walk on water, feed thousands, and heal our fellow man? From the old testament to the new, are we not given many different Gods, distinctly different in nature? God manifests in many forms. Let us not forget that God is the source of *all* that is.

Let me be clear: This is not a God complex that I am offering you. You are not *the* one and only Creator, no more than you are *the* Universe. But you *are* a part of the Universe, a part of the whole, and therefore, what I believe to be, a part of God. The power of creation resides within you, just as it does within all.

There is a source of energy that flows through everyone and everything, the same source of energy that gives matter to all of creation. It is this source of energy that started it all. The first subatomic particle that expanded to create everyone and everything, little god-like fragments, that continue to expand to create the ever-growing, limitless Universe in which we are a part of.

The Big Bang is the leading scientific explanation for how the Universe came to be. According to scientists, it all started from a single point of existence, one tiny ball of energy, that expanded and continues to expand in an infinite nature to create everything we see, hear, touch, smell, and feel all around us, *including you*.

For now, let's call this tiny ball of energy that is responsible for expanding to create the entire Universe, God, as this aligns with most of the great religions of the world, as well as most spiritual teachings, that claim we are all created by the same source, connected by origin. Most of these teachings so often come back to the fact that *we are all one*.

Regardless of what you want to call this Source that started it all, you are an extension of it, a fragment of it, stardust manifested in human form. And just as the bible states that you were created in God's image, you, too, were created in the Universe's image. If you were to compare the veins in the palm of a human hand to the veins found on a leaf, or the radial patterns of human irises to the swirling, cloud-like patterns of nebula in the sky, or an image of neurons in the human brain to images of galaxies, you would find that they are so similar in their likeness; they are often indistinguishable to the eye.

The same geometric shapes and patterns are found throughout the Universe – in nature, in science, music, math, art, and in the physical world that we create. For example, the spiral or swirling energy used in the shaping of flower patterns, shells, whirlpools, and spinning galaxies, is identical to our own DNA. The golden ratio, or phi, is found among many different creatures, forms, objects, and substances in the Universe, from the Pyramids in Egypt, to the tiniest speck of a grain of sand, to the human body.

At our core, we are all made of the same thing – the same subatomic particles that make up the leaf, the sky, and the galaxies, make up you and I.

You are an extension of the energy source that started it all. And just as the Universe is infinitely expanding, always creating, so are you. You, too, have the power to create – to create miracles, to create life, to *create entire worlds* through your consciousness. This energy source is within you, just as it is within all beings and all things.

Much like you, a single droplet of water may seem so small and powerless by itself, but when it connects with all the other droplets of water, it can *become* the ocean. Together, these droplets of water can create entire worlds and can change the course of history. United, they give life to millions of different plants and animals, feed billions of people, produce half of the world's oxygen, and have the ability to create waves so powerful they can knock down buildings, and even destroy entire cities. Just as that droplet of water is not alone on its quest to become, you, too, are not alone in yours. You, too, are connected to all that is.

The interconnectedness of all things can be observed in many different areas of science, including physics, biology, and ecology. Physics tells us that at the subatomic level, particles are connected. The food web in biology illustrates how all living organisms are connected through their relationships with other organisms. Known as ecological connectivity, all ecosystems on Earth are interconnected through the movements of water, air, nutrients, plants, animals, and other living organisms.

This is the main notion behind the butterfly effect, a scientific concept that evokes the idea that even a small butterfly flapping its wings could, hypothetically, cause a typhoon. Our actions affect everyone and everything around us. Because it is *all* connected – *we* are all connected. And this is where our power comes – from our connection to all that is.

Hold your faith in the realm of infinite possibility and make decisions from this place. Always remember that *within you all things are possible*. You are a powerful, almighty being with an energetic force within that is capable of creating magic, capable of using science that is still yet far beyond our understanding.

You were created in God's image to create as God creates. You can *do* anything you want to do. You can *be* anything you want to be. You are *creating* the world around you.

If you can hold a vision in your mind's eye, you can bring it into reality, no matter how crazy or impossible it may seem. And in fact, I believe you are here to create that image that you see within you.

The Beauty of Life

Life is not fair. You likely heard this when you were a child anytime things didn't go your way or you didn't get what you wanted. This saying certainly rings true, as you see bad things happen to good people all the time. You can look around and see lack and want, while others have more than enough. You can see sickness while there is health, and pain while there is pleasure.

But while life may seem unfair based on our individual, unique experiences, and the timing of them, one could argue that the energy source found within us is not. After all, we will *all* experience adversity, heartbreak, sickness, pain, and death at some point. We will experience every human emotion that there is to experience. I like to think this is by design, as it seems true appreciation is only found in the contrast. *This is perhaps the beauty of life.* It is why we love so deeply, why we dream so big, and why we find so much strength in faith – because we have all experienced the lack of these – the *lack* of love, hope, and faith at some point in our lives.

I do not believe our individual blessings and hardships are due to God playing favorites, choosing to save some and not others, determining who is more worthy, more virtuous, or more deserving than another, and thus treating us discriminately. I believe our experiences to be unique only in that they uniquely qualify us for, and push us toward, the connections, the lessons, and the gifts that we are meant to share with the world. I believe the pain you go through is preparing you for who you are meant to be and that everything is actually happening *for* you, not *to* you.

This is not an original thought. As Seneca, a Stoic philosopher of the first century, stated, "A gem cannot be polished without friction, nor a man perfected without trials." It is in the friction that we learn who we truly are.

I believe we are all equal parts of the whole and we all have unique talents to share. I believe there is something you can do that no one else can do *quite* like you. And I believe this is why you are here.

Winston Churchill once famously said, "There comes a special moment in everyone's life, a moment for which that person was born. That special opportunity, when he seizes it, will fulfill his mission – a mission for which he is uniquely qualified. In that moment, he will find greatness. It is his finest hour." I think this quote resonated with people so deeply because we all subconsciously know, deep down to our soul, that it is true.

We spoke of miracles and creation in the previous sections. Now, I'd like you to consider the miracle of *you.* Let's begin with some facts about our planet. Our planet is one of an estimated 100 billion planets in our galaxy, which is estimated to be only one of at least a trillion other galaxies. This brings the total number of planets in the Universe to be somewhere between 70 quintillion to 100 sextillion. I'm not even sure what those numbers mean, nor do I have any way of conceptualizing them, but let's keep going…

Among all of these planets, ours is the only one that we know of that has the right combination of chemicals, water, temperatures, and so forth to support planetary life as we know it. The odds of *this* are thought to be somewhere between one in a million million to one in a trillion trillion.

The fact that we are all walking around on a giant rock suspended in space, spinning on its axis, hurtling through space at a blazing 140 miles per second, while having the perfect conditions to not only hold us to its surface, but to sustain our very existence, and create such living, breathing beauty all around us, is no doubt, a miracle.

But let's take it even more micro than this. Consider the odds of your father meeting your mother on a planet of over 8 billion people, which had to happen generation after generation of similar coincidences in order to create the exact you that stands here today. Consider the sheer number of sperm it takes, somewhere between 80 and 300 million, for just *one* to reach and fertilize *one* of 300 – 500,000 eggs to create your *exact* DNA. Not to be morbid, but when you also factor in the number of miscarriages, stillbirths, and neonatal loss, the fact that you were not only born, but survived, is something like 1 in 400 trillion. Life is a miracle. *You* are a miracle.

You are here for a reason. And there is only *one* you. Scientists say evolution never follows the same path as there are simply too many variables. Your uniqueness, therefore, is a scientific fact. We have a unique genetic makeup where no two individuals will ever be the same, not now, not a million years ago, and not in a million years from now. There will never be another you. When you consider the fact that there have been over one hundred billion humans that have walked the face of this earth to date and not a single one of them is *exactly* like you, you cannot deny that you *are*, indeed, special.

The deepest desires in your heart are not random. I believe your desires are your destiny – they are your calling. There is a reason why one person can write an incredible book and another can make an incredible pot of soup. There is a reason why one person loves children, and another loves medicine, and another plants, and another design, and another coaching, and another painting.

No two people have the exact same dream, or feel the exact same call. There are subtleties and intricacies and ways of perceiving, and being, and expressing that are unique to each of us. And when we are all living up to our highest potential, and using the energetic power we hold within to bring forth the unique vision within, we are fulfilling our mission. We are doing our equal part in the creation of the perfect Universe, on Earth as it is in heaven. *This* is God realized.

The word desire comes from the latin word desiderare, which means "heavenly body". It is in the pursuit of your desires that you create heaven on Earth. The only true satisfaction in life is found in cultivating purpose and passion and pursuing that with which we love. When we remove our belief in the possibility of this, we see and feel the effects all around us.

As Philippians 4:8 states, "Idle minds are the devil's playground." That voice in your head that tells you to give up on your dreams is the metaphorical devil on your shoulder – your ego, which is rooted not in unity, but in separateness, telling you that you are separate from those who are able to create their dreams, telling you that you do not deserve, cannot have, or are not good enough to lead the life you desire to live.

In the Gospel of Thomas it states, "If you bring forth what is within you, what you bring forth will save you. If you do not bring forth what is within you, what you do not bring forth will destroy you." When the ego wins, separation wins. You become separate from everyone and everything. You begin living in a lie. Thus, your relationships suffer, your mind suffers, your physical body suffers, and the *world* suffers. You are, for all intents and purposes, living your own personal hell. This unfortunately is many people's realities.

But *nothing* could be further from the truth. The truth is that it is not God that creates poverty, famine, drought, or disease, it is man, not living up to his full potential. It is man, focusing on the problems, and creating more of them. It is man, believing in scarcity and creating more of it. It is man, putting money on a pedestal rather than his own power to create. It is man, looking without, rather than looking within. It is man praying to God to save him, rather than choosing to save himself.

You are here to create the vision you see within and all can be saved *in a single moment* when you make the decision to begin following the vision within instead of the noise without. *This* is how you save *yourself.* And this is why I believe God to not be a being, but rather found in *being* oneself.

I believe we already have all the tools and resources available to us that are necessary to make our own unique dreams come true, to create whatever it is that we desire, to do our part in creating a world filled with purpose, and passion, and love. We need only tune in to the reality of it, to be able to perceive it, as it goes beyond the physical senses.

According to scientific findings, a tiny 1% of the electromagnetic spectrum on Earth is able to be perceived by the human eye. The other 99% is not visible to us. What is found within that other 99% that we are oblivious to? All that we know about the invisible spectrum is that it contains a vast range of energy beyond our senses.

I picture 100 layers of reality, all interlaid upon one another. And here we are in the first layer, completely oblivious to all the other layers simultaneously happening within our world, yet outside of our perception. Are there spirits floating along beside us? Are there angels whispering in our ears? Are there aliens zipping in and out of our atmosphere?

No one knows for sure. But we do know that we live in an ever-expanding, infinite Universe. And if you ask me, I think it is pure potential and possibility, the infiniteness that we *know* exists but cannot directly observe. I believe that 99% of reality is pure magic that we can only access using the power of belief found deep within.

"So we fix our eyes not on what is seen, but on what is unseen, since what is seen is temporary, but what is unseen is eternal." Corinthians 4:18. The fact that you are able to perceive the vision within, when no one else in the world can, is the only proof you need that you were designed to carry it out. Nothing that comes into your 1% awareness is insignificant. The fact that you are able to perceive the idea, to think about it at all, means that it is not only possible for you, but that it is *meant* for you.

Be Still and Know that I am God

"The Kingdom of God is within you." - Luke 17:21

Within you there is a gentle, guiding voice that does not originate in your intellectual mind, but deep within. It often presents itself and is heard the loudest when the mind is completely still and quiet.

Some attribute this voice to be that of God, the holy spirit, your soul, your conscience, or perhaps your higher self. And to all of these, I would say, yes – absolutely, it *is* all of these. But for the sake of keeping things simple, let's just call it your intuition.

An experiment in the journal *Science*, which was conducted by Dr. Damasio, a neuroscientist at the University of Iowa College of Medicine, found that a person's intuition knows things before the mind can perceive it.

The experiment gave participants four decks of cards in which each card was either worth a sum of money or a penalty, and the participants were asked to try to win as much money as they could. The game had been rigged so that two decks were "good decks" in that they produced lower immediate rewards but higher total payout, and two decks were "bad decks" in which they gave the thrill of large earnings but greater losses. After turning about 50 cards, most participants reached the correct conclusion, that two decks were good and two decks were bad, even though the bad decks often had higher payouts.

However, before their conscious mind came to this conclusion, the players began playing advantageously, choosing to pull from the good deck a majority of the time, far before they had enough evidence to figure out that the decks were rigged. Not only that, but their bodies gave tell-tale signs that they intuitively understood which decks were good and which decks were bad each time they reached for a pile.

There have been other studies such as this that have come to the same scientific conclusion, that intuition is not only quicker than our conscious minds at picking up on things, but that it is far more accurate. We simply *know* things within.

Intuition is defined in the dictionary as "the ability to acquire direct knowledge without recourse to conscious reasoning." I direct your attention to the word "conscious" to reiterate that this knowing, this intuition, comes from the subconscious. Remember that your RAS, the gatekeeper to your conscious mind, is taking in millions of bits of data every second, filtering only a nano amount into your conscious awareness.

That means that the subconscious must hold infinitely more intelligence than the conscious mind. And *you* have access to it. I like to think of this as the ability to tap into the quantum, or the world of infinite knowledge, abilities, potentials, and possibilities. This is, what I believe to be, your connection to the Universe, your connection to all that is, all that was, and all that will ever be. It is where you find your connection to God, in the stillness within. It is a part of you that is beyond the mind, beyond your awareness of your physical body, and beyond space and time.

The voice of your intuition often comes through without effort, without thinking, and without analyzing. As Albert Einstein once famously said, "I think 99 times and find nothing. I stop thinking, swim in silence, and the truth comes to me...I didn't arrive at my understanding of the fundamental laws of the Universe through my rational mind."

The voice of your intuition may present itself in actual words, visual pictures, a feeling, or it may just render a deep knowing, an instinctual push to take some kind of action or a series of actions.

Just as your RAS's first priority is to keep you and your offspring safe, there are times that these actions can save your life or the life of those you love. The subconscious mind, processing visual and environmental cues, that the conscious mind does not have the capacity for, can trigger a rapid response when it detects a potential threat.

For example, a driver on the highway suddenly senses danger, hitting the brakes instinctively. This quick reaction of the brain sending a signal to the foot, without one's conscious realization, prevents a collision with a vehicle that unexpectedly swerves into their lane a moment later.

A mother is walking around a department store with her child, when she suddenly gets an off-putting feeling in her gut about the man in the aisle next to her. She follows her instincts and grabs her child's hand to keep him/her close for the remainder of the shopping trip. Later, she finds out that a child was abducted from the very store they were in.

This voice can also help lead you to people, places, or things that you are meant to find to better your life or the life of someone else.

This could look like an unexplainable desire to go down a different street than you normally take on your evening walk. On that street you find a wad of cash on the side of the road just in time to pay a bill you didn't know how you were going to pay, or run into a neighbor that becomes a good friend, or see a stray dog that you end up helping to find a home with a family in need of love.

It could also look something like this: Your friend's name, or their face, or something that reminds you of them, comes into your awareness out of nowhere, and you feel a push to call them. Upon calling, you may find that they were actually just thinking about calling you. You may find that they really needed your help. Or, there may be something they tell you during that call that was the answer to something you had been searching for.

Throughout your life, your intuition will try to guide you. But so often, our intuition is drowned out by both external and internal noise. Along with cell phones and radios and television, and other people talking to us and around us, there's also the competing voice within – our ego, or our conscious mind.

Identifying between your intuition and ego is actually quite simple. While your ego produces thoughts and feelings rooted in fear, anger, and separation, your intuition produces only thoughts and feelings rooted in love, joy, and unity.

In the department store and car breaking example above, it is not fear, but a quick, intuitive response of protection, which is rooted in love. An egoic decision, on the other hand, could have been to angrily speed up and overtake the car that slowed down in front of you, not realizing that it did so because it had a view of an accident up ahead that you cannot yet see, or yelling at your child when you can't find them right away in the department store as your mind begins to wonder if they have been taken.

Intuition cannot be easily rationalized or explained. Your body simply knows things before you can fully grasp it with your mind. When you find the voice of your intuition, much like when you find the love of your life, you know right away. I compare it to love because it is the *source* of all love. Like love, it does not originate in the mind – through a string of thoughts compounded upon one another to produce some forlorn conclusion. Instead, it is a simple and concise awareness that is unexplainable, yet undeniable, and perfectly clear. *Just as love is.*

Your intuition will produce only loving thoughts and loving actions and a deep feeling of love for yourself and others. It will always abide by the law of oneness and the law of karma, or the golden rule, to treat others the way you want to be treated. For it is the voice of unity, the connection to all that is. It is, again, what I would call, the voice of God.

There is an old Cherokee Legend which illustrates the battle between the intuition and ego wonderfully. The story goes like this:

"An old Cherokee is teaching his grandson about life.

'A fight is going on inside me,' he said to the little boy.
'It is a terrible fight and it is between two wolves. One
is evil – he is anger, envy, sorrow, regret, greed,
arrogance, self-pity, guilt, resentment, inferiority, lies,
false pride, superiority, and ego.'

He continued, 'The other is good – he is joy, peace,
love, hope, serenity, humility, kindness, benevolence,
empathy, generosity, truth, compassion, and faith. The
same fight is going on inside you – and inside every
other person, too.'

The grandson thought about it for a minute and then
asked his grandfather, 'Which wolf will win?'

The old Cherokee simply replied, 'The one you feed.'"

76

Feed the good wolf. Take Psalm 46:10, "Be still and know that I am God," and follow its guidance. Make it a practice to slow down and find that still place within, know that this is where you find God. "The spirit of God dwells within you." 1 Corinthians 3:16.

Meditating for a few minutes a day will bring you closer to God than any church, or teacher, or book ever could. Practice separating yourself from your thoughts, or your ego, and begin observing rather than judging them, and you will gain more clarity in your life than any amount of research or advice could ever give you. As Albert Einstein said, "The intuitive mind is a sacred gift and the rational mind a faithful servant. We have created a society that honors the servant and has forgotten the gift." Don't be like the rest of society. Choose to honor your gift.

Meditation has been proven to reduce anxiety, stress, depression, loneliness, and pain, to improve sleep, heart health, and immunity. It decreases blood pressure, supports mental health, aids in curing addictions, enhances memory, cognitive skills, self-awareness, and focus. It promotes healthy emotions, creativity, and kindness. All of this has been proven scientifically through thousands of experiments. What else can you name that single handedly produces this array of life-changing results? Is this not miraculous? Is it not divine? And it is all within *you*.

I believe that the bible got this one right. Heaven *is* on Earth. It is within each and every one of us. To find it, one must only find stillness. Listen to the kingdom of God within. When seeking answers, rather than asking outside of yourself, find a quiet place, take a few deep breaths, and ask the voice within for guidance instead. As Jeremiah, verse 29:11 states, "For I know the plans I (God) have for you." Your intuition, the God within, simply *knows*.

You can ask your intuition any question and it will produce a loving answer. You can ask for its direction anytime and it will provide you with an optimal path toward your desires. The more you intentionally connect to your intuition and ask for, as well as follow the guidance you receive, the louder this voice of knowing will become. It will become the guiding force in your life letting you know what is truly meant for you and what is wrong for you.

As the Lao Tzu states, "To a mind that is still, the whole Universe surrenders."

Below is a simple practice for getting in touch with your intuition:

Ask yourself a *yes* or *no* question that you already know the answer to and feel where and how the *yes* and *no* shows up in your body. Use a statement, rather than a question, as it is easier for your subconscious mind to respond to.

Find a quiet place where you will not be interrupted, close your eyes, and take ten to fifteen deep and full breaths in and out, focusing only on your breath. Follow with a statement out loud that you already know, without a doubt, that the answer to is *no*, such as: *Drinking alcohol every day is good for me.*

Then tune in to your body. It will likely give you an immediate response. Where do you feel the *no*? For me, I feel the *no* deep down in my gut, and it is a contracting feeling, rather than an expanding feeling. It feels dense and heavy. Your *no* may be in a different place and produce a different feeling. But once you get it, you now know that this is your intuition's way of communicating that something is not right for you.

Now follow the same routine, making another statement that you for sure know that the answer is a *yes*. For example: *Being in nature is good for me.* Where do you feel the *yes*? For me, I feel the *yes* in my chest, as if it is a heart response. It is an expanding, thrilling feeling, as if my heart is opening up. Your *yes* may be in a different area of your body and produce a different feeling. But once you find it, you now know that this is your intuition's way of communicating that something is a *yes* for you.

Once you know the feeling produced by a *yes* and *no* answer, you can begin asking yourself simple questions each day. Continue to keep the questions in statement form, rather than question form. For example, you can make statements daily, such as: *I should go on a walk this morning. I should wear this shirt today. I should stop for a coffee this morning. I should go to the party.* Keep it simple at first as you build up your trust in your intuition. Then you can move on to bigger statements, such as: *I should find a different job. I should break up with my boyfriend. I should start this project now.*

Another easy way to begin intentionally connecting to your intuition is through automatic writing. This is actually how I began communicating with my intuition and have received life-changing advice on many occasions. It was this method that led me to step down from my training position at work several years after my promotion when I was overwhelmed with stress and plagued with severe digestive issues.

I had never considered giving up my training position because *I liked it* – I *liked* the money, I *liked* the feeling of importance, and I *liked* teaching. But what I didn't realize until my intuition guided me to it was that I didn't *love* it and it was taking away from what I *did love*. I had no extra time to do all the things I loved to do.

I had never tied the stress from work to my digestive issues. When I read back what I had written in response to the question, *why is my stomach hurting all the time*, I was shocked. It wasn't my words, but some deep knowing within, guiding me to do what was best for me when I didn't even consciously know what was best for me.

Once I followed the advice and stepped down from my position, relief flooded my body, and I felt a weight lift off my chest. A string of events followed that led to me finding a cure for my symptoms which I would have never stumbled upon had I not listened to my intuition's advice, which allowed me to be in the right place at the right time.

Had I not stepped down from my position at work I wouldn't have been exactly where I needed to be in the exact moment that I was, right in the middle of a work day. I would have been too busy to have been on that walk, to have been fully immersed in the moment and open to a hit of inspiration to reach out to a friend, who would then provide me with the answers I had been seeking.

It is said that God works in mysterious ways, and I believe this to be true. Often, the advice you receive does not make rational sense at the time and can only be understood when looking backward. It is only in looking back now that I see quitting my role as a trainer served a far greater purpose in my life than just healing my stomach.

Had I listened to my ego, rather than my intuition that day, I would have continued along the path to partner. I would have no doubt accepted the management position that was offered to me a year later, which I instead promptly turned down after asking my intuition again if it was right for me. I would have been working 50+ hour weeks, the work piling higher and higher on my desk each day, with an office of employees relying heavily on me, and in extreme physical pain still, all while experiencing what was about to be the greatest tragedy of my life.

By following my intuition, and strengthening the trust I had in my inner knowing, I was able to fully be there for my mom and dad, and Shawn and the kids, when they needed me the most. I was able to make the phone calls for Shawn that he simply could not handle. I was able to pack up and move in to help him and the kids. I was able to do the things I would have no doubt done anyway, but without all of the stress that had caused me so much pain in the first place. There is no telling where my health would be today had I not checked in with myself.

Dr. Andrew Newburg, a neuroscientist conducted studies on the brain while people practiced automatic writing and found that the frontal lobe, the area of the brain associated with critical and creative thinking, actually powers down during this practice. It is as if your brain goes offline. So, the information flowing from your fingertips has been scientifically proven to not come from your mind, but perhaps somewhere else deep within you.

If you choose to connect with your intuition and strengthen your trust in your inner knowing by following the advice you receive, you, too, will often find yourself in the right place at the right time, and your life will improve in ways you could have never imagined.

Take out your journal, find a quiet place, take a few deep breaths, and then write a question at the top of the paper. Let your pen flow, writing everything that comes immediately into your mind, without judgement and without analyzing. Keep asking follow-up questions as they come. Wait to read it back until you feel as though you are finished and have gotten your answer.

Remember, the key with this is to not think, but to let whatever comes through you to flow onto the page. When you read it back, you may be surprised at the advice you receive. While it has come from your pen, it may not sound like your words, and will often be in opposition to your egoic mind.

Just as the beginning of the verse says, "Be Still and KNOW," trust your deep inner knowing above all else. Practice complete and unwavering, unyielding faith in the truth you find within and follow the guidance you receive.

You will have reached mastery over your life when the voice of your intuition becomes louder than that of your ego in the moments of the everyday. You, too, can make this your reality with a little practice, and a lot of trust.

I Am...

Perhaps the most significant part of this verse, "Be still and know that I am God," is the second part of it. To master harnessing the power within, take a look in the mirror as you repeat it to yourself.

"I am" are the single two most powerful words in the Universe. Do not put anything after "I am" that is not worthy of God. Be careful and intentional about what you put after these two words because they *will* create the you that is reflected back to you.

Affirmations, or what some may call prayers, are about affirming your desires within, not begging God for what you want. Research has found that by repeating affirmations, you activate and strengthen neural pathways in your brain associated with the affirmation's message. This is again, called neural plasticity. In essence, you are rewiring your brain, and thus, becoming someone new, and creating a new reality.

As Muhammad Ali said, "It's the repetition of affirmations that lead to belief. And once that belief becomes a deep conviction, things begin to happen." The repetition of these ideas is a signal to your subconscious that it is not only important to you, but that it is *true* for you. Your brain will begin looking for the proof in your external reality to align with your internal beliefs.

You are the creator of your reality. Do not let your self-talk create a *you* that is powerless. Do not create a *you* that has blocks, boundaries, and limitations. Do not create a *you* that is capable of anything less than what you truly desire.

"As a man thinks in his heart, so he is." Proverbs 23:7.

I am healthy. I am happy. I am loved. I am abundant. And so, you are.

I am going to give the best speech of my life. I am going to find the love of my life. I am going to buy my dream home. I am going to become a millionaire. And so, you do.

I am...I am...I am... And so, you create.

With God, all things are possible, and therefore, within *you* all things are possible. Design your life accordingly.

John 1:1-4 states, "In the beginning was the Word, and the Word was with God, and the Word was God himself. All things were made and came into existence through Him; and without Him, not even one thing was made that has come into being."

The Word was God himself. Your words are God himself. Just as Muhammad Ali claimed he was the greatest before he actually was, and called forth that reality. Just as I said out loud that I truly believed I'd be a millionaire one day, and it came to be. Claim your desires as already yours, without hesitation, without fear, without proof. Imagine your deepest desires coming true as if they already have, and then move forth as if they are inevitable, and you will draw out the resources needed to create them.

I'd like to point out here that in the original bible written in Greek, "logos", from which we get the word logic, was roughly translated into "the word." However, if you take the actual translation of the word logos, as according to the book *Alpha to Omega*, it is the outward expression of a concept *and* the actual concept itself. Thoughts are the building blocks of creation and everything you see around you began as a thought. It is the outward expression of those thoughts that is creation itself. And in order to outwardly express your thoughts, you must believe in them.

"According to your faith, shall it be done to you." Matthew 9:29. Know, without a doubt, that what you want is already on its way to you and declare it as so. Be so sure of it that you speak of it. Be so sure of it that you act on it.

The magic is in the knowing. It is in the knowing, *especially* in the last hour, when the illusion of impossibility is at its strongest, that faith prevails. So many people give up on their dreams when they are at the one-yard line. So many people give up faith when their desire is right on the other side of their fear, or on the other side of their failure. I believe this is by divine design, as the desire must be true for you to keep believing, and to keep striving, even when all is seemingly lost.

And when all is lost, that is when your continued faith can move mountains. "Truly I tell you, if you have faith as small as a mustard seed, you can say to this mountain, 'Move from here to there,' and it will move. Nothing will be impossible for you." Matthew 17:20.

Nothing is impossible for you. Follow the intuitive, inspired actions as they come and you will create a life beyond your wildest dreams as well. You will finally be *free.*

"I took a deep breath and listened to the old brag of my heart. I am, I am, I am..."

Sylvia Plath

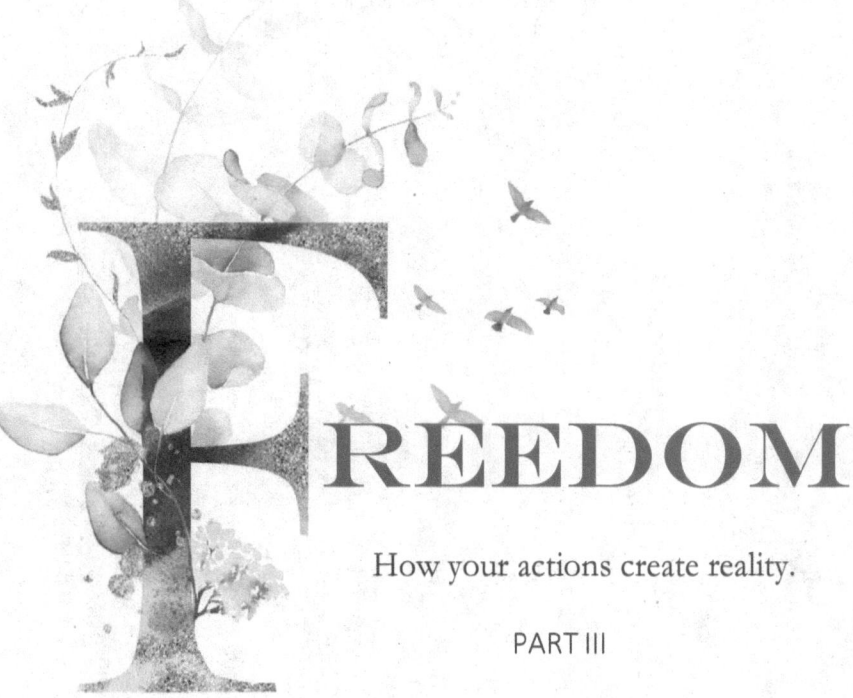

FREEDOM

How your actions create reality.

PART III

Free-dom

\<noun\>

The power to act, speak, or think as one wants without hindrance or restraint.

NEW OXFORD AMERICAN DICTIONARY

PART 3: FREEDOM

"If one advances confidently in the direction of his dreams, and endeavors to live the life which he has imagined, he will meet with a success unexpected in common hours."

While Shawn's faith certainly felt like it played a pivotal role in his eventual freedom, it seemed as though it were his actions that solidified his faith into reality.

Shawn didn't just hold onto his faith within, but moved ahead as if his freedom were inevitable, taking actions that aligned with his desire to *be* free, as if he *already was* free. Not once did he stop and say, "let's do this, just in case", or "let's hold off on this until after the trial", or "let's wait until we know for sure what is going to happen".

No, he changed the channel on that potential reality entirely. He woke up every single day and assumed his freedom by making plans for and working toward that freedom. Through his actions, he tuned into and became a vibrational match to freedom. And he continued to do this even when his lawyers began preparing him for the worst.

Shawn could have given up on his freedom based on his fears, or on very real historical precedence, or on the advice or opinions of others who knew far more than he did about the law, long before his trial. He could have convicted himself guilty in his mind and put bars around his actions before ever receiving a verdict.

But he didn't. He held onto his own free will, to the creative power he held over his life, and created so much momentum behind his desire to be free that it was as if reality had no choice but to calibrate to the massive actions he was taking. I believe this was because his *why*, the love he had for his children, was far more powerful than his fear.

In the aftermath of my sister's death, I took back the power of freedom over my own life as well. While my prison was entirely metaphorical, I realized that I had been putting self-imposed bars around my actions my entire life. It wasn't until tragedy struck, and I realized how quickly life could be over, that I realized this.

Like everyone else I knew, I was spending the majority of my time working. Not just working, but *excelling* at my job. And for what? For maybe an extra 1% or 2% raise each year as compared to my co-worker's raises? For my boss's praise and admiration? For promotions and job offers that I didn't even really want?

These were all ego-based desires. None of these things really mattered. I had been conditioned to believe they did, but other than the very fleeting feeling of superiority I received in these moments of recognition, not a single one of them actually contributed to my overall happiness or fulfillment. And yet, I'd been acting as though my job was my number one priority, the most important thing in my life. I had been allowing it to dictate how I spent every single moment of every single day, scheduling everything else around it.

I remembered how grateful I had felt when my boss allowed me to take a week off in the middle of our busy season to attend my sister's wedding in the Dominican Republic. Even though I was always way ahead in my work and would have everything complete that I needed to before the trip, I had actually been afraid that my request for time off wouldn't get approved.

Now that the veil had been lifted, I realized how insane this was. I realized how insane it was that I would be willing to miss a once-in-a-lifetime moment if my boss said that I couldn't attend. I realized how insane it was that my favorite season of the year was Fall, and because our biggest deadline of the year was in the middle of October, I missed the best parts of my favorite season every single year. I was required to work extra hours for no extra pay, not because I was behind on my work, but because others were behind on theirs.

Even when I did finally make it outside to enjoy the crisp, cool breeze of fall, the crunch of leaves under my feet, and the beautiful changing colors of the season, I was under so much pressure and stress that I couldn't even enjoy it. I had allowed myself to become responsible for rushing to complete work last minute for other people's clients when there was an inadequate amount of time left to do it completely or accurately. I stressed over the quality of my work and the looming deadline, which left me dreading my favorite season every year.

Clearly, I had lost my mind. That was the only explanation I could come up with. I'd been so brainwashed into believing that my job was my number one priority, apparently the only job out there, that I'd completely negated the fact that I was in a power position at work. They needed *me*, I didn't *need* them. And yet, I had allowed myself to be walked all over.

I could suddenly see so clearly how little of a priority my job was in the grand scheme of things. Yes, it helped pay the bills and afford us a decent life, but it wasn't the end-all, be-all, for that decent life. I could always find another job if I needed to.

And if I did? If I left my company, all of my hard work would be forgotten. None of it would even matter anymore. When I moved on to another job or retired, I wouldn't even *think* about all the work I'd done there. It would mean absolutely nothing to me. How could that be, that something I would spend my entire life working on, the vast majority of my every day, could be so inconsequential to me in the end?

I also realized that if I made my dreams come true, *when* I made my dreams come true, as that was now what I was choosing to whole-heartedly believe would happen, my job would soon become my last priority by default, as I would inevitably quit to write full-time anyway.

Once I came to the realization that this new life of mine meant quitting my job, it was quite easy to put it last on my list of priorities and to throw my old life and old schedule completely out the window to start anew. I created a new schedule for myself – I decided that every morning when I'd sit down to work, I'd do the most important thing first – the most important thing according to *my* priorities, not anyone else's. I would turn off my phone's ringer and email notifications, without fail, regardless of how much work I had to do. I would set my status to "do not disturb", and I would write. I would write until I was tired of writing, which typically meant somewhere between two and three hours.

I worked from home and had been with my company for close to ten years. So, based on my tenure and track record, I was able to get away with this fairly easily. Logically, I knew that even if I got caught not working when I was supposed to be, it would take a lot for me to get fired. I had seen people that really *needed* to be fired, *not* get fired, for years. Plus, I had years of knowledge and experience that they would not want to throw away over some rough patch I might be going through.

But the truth was, even if it came down to that, I just couldn't care less anymore. Losing my sister had put everything into perspective for me. I could see so clearly now that my job *really was* my last priority. I had new priorities now, based on *my own* desires, not someone else's. And honestly, I dared someone to say something to me about it. It was so crystal clear to me now how much I had allowed myself to be taken advantage of over the years. Since I was reliable and always got everything done that was put in front of me, they'd continued to pile more and more work on me, making my job and life far more stressful than it needed to be.

But not anymore. I was no longer going to allow it. I would start saying no to helping my co-workers and to additional projects. Would that ruffle some feathers? I was sure of it. But did I care? Not anymore. What were they going to do, fire me?

I decided I'd stop working ahead and only get done what was necessary *when* it was necessary. I would take advantage of the fact that what took someone else eight hours to do, only took me four, and would stop filling those other four hours with extra work. After all, they weren't paying me for my hours worked, they were paying me a salary for my years of experience and ability to do the job, no matter how much time it took me. They certainly didn't pay me overtime when I worked *more* hours. This was the truth of the situation, and thinking about it any other way than this was giving all of my power away to an entity that didn't show me nearly as much respect as I showed it.

With this rearranging of my priorities and shift in my daily habits, reality itself seemed to rearrange and shift as well.

I'll never forget one morning that I unknowingly missed several calls from my boss. I didn't return the calls until I had finished writing *three hours later*. I braced myself for the questions to come about where I had been and why I had taken so long to get back to her. Instead, she didn't miss a beat, going straight into what she needed from me, not even giving the time that had elapsed a second thought.

Not only did no one ever question me about where I was or what I was doing every morning, but since I was no longer answering the phone on the first ring, people stopped contacting me for help constantly. I had stepped down from my position as a trainer, but the relationships had already been developed, and people felt comfortable with me, so I was still always the first call when anyone needed help. After a couple of weeks of turning my ringer on silent and not returning calls right away, people just stopped calling. They started reaching out to each other instead. In addition, since I was only doing what absolutely had to be done each day, I was no longer way ahead of my coworkers, so the extra work stopped coming.

By setting clear boundaries for myself about what I was available for and taking actions that aligned with those boundaries, it was as though everyone else got on board too – silently agreeing with my boundaries, without me even having to say anything. As I became less available to others, I suddenly had all this extra time available to *me*. And, as I reduced the time I spent working, the work *itself* seemed to reduce as well.

As I put less importance on my work and thus spent less time on it, I also found that I was somehow completing my work in a fraction of the time it took me before. What used to never seem finished, now was complete in only a couple of hours a day. Work was not just less time-consuming, it seemed to have become easier too. As I stopped worrying about work so much, work *became* less worrisome. Once I removed my focus from it, it was as though it shapeshifted into something else entirely.

Instead, it had become almost *joyful* to do my work. After writing for a few hours each morning, I was on a high, my cup overflowing. When I sat down to finally complete the tasks I needed to, I was doing so from a place of joy, and I was sailing through them with ease.

I felt a sense of fulfillment unlike any other I had ever felt before. Although nothing on the surface had really changed with my work situation, it *felt* as though it already had. And while I certainly wasn't a best-selling author yet, it *felt* as though I already was. I already spent my mornings writing, just as I'd imagined I would if I were the author I dreamed of being. I already felt the passion and purpose that I had been yearning for in wanting to become an author in the first place. Building toward that future felt just as good as I imagined that the future, itself, would feel. It began to feel inevitable as I put in the work each day, proving to myself that I could do it.

The shift in my priorities and daily habits was not just shifting my mindset, reinforcing my faith in the future, but also shifting my outer reality as well. The open time in my days seemed to keep growing, as well as my freedom. I was finding the time to do all kinds of other things I wanted to do, things I would do if I already was a best-selling author and didn't have a full-time job. I was finding the time to go on walks during the day, to cook, to work out, even to read books I had been wanting to read for years. It was as if I was *somehow* creating more time in my days, just by putting less importance on my work and doing more of what I loved to do.

I was doing things that I really shouldn't have had the time to do. I was creating my book when I shouldn't have had the time to create it. I was becoming a writer, when I really shouldn't have had the time to write. And then, something truly magical happened.

On May 3, 2022, my second baby, Khloe Rose Littrell, was born. Twelve weeks later, when I was scheduled to go back to work from Maternity Leave, I realized that work wasn't just my last priority in my *mind* anymore, but that it had actually become my last priority in *reality*. We no longer needed the income from my job. My husband's logistics company had taken off and he was on track to make a million-dollar profit for the year.

While I had played a part in the business since its inception, taking care of much of the administrative work, he now needed me more than ever. The company was growing quicker than he could keep up with and he needed someone he could trust to hand off more to so that he could free up his time to focus on what he did best. It made sense for me to quit my job so that I could fully focus on the family business, and use the additional free time to pursue *my* dream. After all, I had supported my husband in realizing his dreams for years, and now the stars had aligned for him to support me in realizing mine.

A year and a half after making the decision that my job was my last priority, and forging ahead as though it were, reality shifted and aligned with my actions, as it *truly* became my last priority, something I no longer wanted or needed in my life.

A year and a half after making the decision that I was going to fulfill my dream of becoming a writer, and forging ahead along that path, reality shifted and aligned with my actions, and here I sat with an open schedule to write as much as I wanted to every single day.

I had *become* a writer. I suddenly had complete and total freedom, just as I'd always dreamed of. And now, here *you* are, reading my first book. My dream, manifested.

What had started only in my mind, became anchored into reality once it was backed with action. Once I finally made the decision and took the steps to rearrange my schedule to focus on my dreams, everything shifted. The alignment of my thoughts, beliefs, and actions had created an unstoppable momentum in which everything seemed to come into congruence. The longer I held on to the vibration of freedom, the more dominant the vibration became, as if pulling everything around me into resonance with it. I had tuned into a new frequency and reality met me there.

Quantum leaps don't always happen fast. As a matter of fact, they typically are not fast, *until* they are. I know that doesn't make much sense, but stay with me here. I dreamed of being a writer my entire life, so to finally have written my first book and to be writing full time by age 38 seems more like a painstakingly slow progression rather than a quantum leap. But as you now know, once everything came into alignment – my thoughts, beliefs, and actions – it seemed as though it took no time at all, as if it happened all at once. I had kept my eye on the future version of me, had showed up as her each and every day, and sooner than I could have ever imagined, the future was upon me.

This was true for my husband, Kyle, as well, as he dreamed of being an entrepreneur his entire life. It took him *nine years* of action to find the success he had been searching for. Nevertheless, he experienced a massive quantum leap too, once *his* thoughts, beliefs, and actions all finally came into alignment as well.

Kyle's journey to success began shortly after graduating college with a marketing degree when he got a call from a recruiter about a job opportunity with a local marketing firm. The organization claimed to work with only Fortune 500 clients and presented itself as the ultimate entrepreneurial opportunity for the right candidate. If he was able to prove himself in the marketing and promotion of their client's products, he could move up the ladder, and potentially open his own office as they signed on new clients and expanded into new territories.

For someone like Kyle, who was ambitious and ready to take on the world, this was music to his ears. It seemed to him as if he'd just been handed a treasure map with the "X" clearly marked; a straightforward and easy-to-navigate path toward ultimate freedom. If he followed their path to success, he could own his own business – something he'd always dreamed about.

Kyle went through three interviews before he was finally offered the job. In his first interview, he was told to go home and come back in a suit if he wanted to be taken seriously.

In his second interview, he was told about the money. In addition to the commission and raises one could expect while moving up the ladder, there were also company-paid trips around the country to see other markets, and retreats to tropical paradises for owners and outstanding sales reps. He was told that owners in the company made well over six-figures and some of the more talented reps became owners in less than a year.

In his third interview, he was grilled about his work ethic and desire to become an entrepreneur. Did he have the grit? Was he willing to put in the hard work now for the big pay-off later?

Each morning, as Kyle had sat waiting to be interviewed, he could overhear the employees in their morning meeting. The atmosphere was one of energy and enthusiasm, with lots of whooping, and hollering, and bells being rung. It sounded like one big celebration. As the employees dispersed, he couldn't miss how professional and sharp they all looked, as though they were rolling in money. Everyone seemed to be go-getters, excited about the opportunity they had, and happy to be a part of such a great company.

Kyle was immediately sold. When he was offered a job at the ground level, in the position of "Trainee", which was what he was told everyone started out at, he was ecstatic.

While the recruiter and the interviewer glorified the opportunity, focusing the conversation on how quickly he could become an owner and the money that was to eventually be made, they skirted around the actual day-to-day job duties, which consisted of standing in a retail store, propositioning strangers to sign up for television service. There was no actual marketing involved in the entry level position, just direct sales.

Kyle, who never met a stranger and delighted in making new friends, excelled at it. He quickly moved all the way up the ladder, continuing in direct sales every step of the way, but also participating in other aspects of the business as well – interviewing candidates, training and mentoring new employees, and finally, learning the ins and outs of becoming a business owner.

It wasn't long before he was indeed given the opportunity to run his own office. His territory would be four hours away in the small town of West Lafayette, Indiana. There were three big-box retailers under his contract that he would be required to staff with salespeople.

The process to ownership began quickly. Kyle signed the paperwork that day to open an LLC in the business name of his choosing, along with a contract between himself and the organization that was in charge of all of the independent offices, including the one he was being promoted out of. They gave him the name of a recruiter who he could pay to run employment ads and schedule interviews for him, a payroll company he could pay to handle his weekly payroll, and a co-worker who was ready to be promoted that he could take along with him to be his assistant manager – his first employee.

Everything else was up to him to make happen, both logistically and financially. After a quick celebration and a pat on the back, Kyle was sent on his way. He did his part – he found a cheap two-bedroom apartment in the area for himself and his employee to rent, and an even cheaper office space in an old, run-down building. This was meant to do the job intermittently until he started making enough money to be able to afford a better one. He began paying the payroll company, the recruiter, and his assistant manager. Since he had no income yet as a business owner and hadn't made enough as a sales rep to have any kind of savings, these expenses were paid either by loans from his promoting office or with his personal credit card.

As the three stores in his market got a kickback with every sell, they were motivated to have his salespeople in their stores. It was in his contract that he had to keep them staffed six days a week after his initial grace period. Otherwise, he would default on his contract and potentially lose the stores to the next in line for a promotion. The organization also retained the right to shut down his business if he didn't meet their sales goals and expectations.

Thus began a vicious and monotonous wheel of non-stop work. Kyle's schedule looked something like this: Get to the office by seven am to prepare for the morning meeting and complete any paperwork needing to be done. Run through the morning motivational and sales training meeting with his employees to pump them up for the day ahead before sending them off to their store assignments. Conduct first, second, and/or third-round interviews with any potential candidates brought in by his recruiter. And finally, go to a store to either provide hands-on training to the new staff, tag along to mentor and motivate the seasoned staff, provide coverage as it was so often lacking, and *always* to generate more sales to meet his quota for the week.

Despite the looks of his run-down office and Kyle's youthful demeanor, getting new people in the door to sell was not a problem. The recruiter he'd hired from within the company was well-versed in using glittery language to make the job seem like the ultimate opportunity. Kyle was also an extremely likable boss. People wanted to be in his energy. They *wanted* to work for him.

He also followed the same routine as his predecessor and had candidates waiting in the lobby, able to overhear the morning meetings, which were always excessively positive regardless of what was actually going on behind closed doors. All of the staff knew that there were interviewees outside the door and to be on their best behavior. They were motivated to do this, because before anyone could be promoted, they had to replace themselves, and in order to become an eventual owner, they had to develop a team of successful salespeople under them. So, the more the merrier.

However, once new hires saw what was expected of them day-to-day, they were typically out the door before their first week had come to a close. Those that had a natural sales ability and drive would often last a few months, but typically couldn't hold out long enough for promotion because, well, they had bills to pay. Sales reps received a small hourly rate, but worked off of a draw against their commission, which meant if they didn't make enough commission to cover their hourly pay, they had to pay back the amount they had essentially "borrowed" before they were able to be paid commission again. As you can imagine, this kept them constantly in the hole, trying to dig their way out of the red so that they could actually take home a commission check.

Despite these difficult working conditions, a select few stayed in it for the long haul, those with a sparkle in their eye like Kyle, focused on the treasure at the end of the long, arduous journey; the carrot of entrepreneurship that was constantly being dangled in front of them. But even with having a few of those long-term employees that he could count on, it didn't keep the store's long hours completely staffed. And while the goal for Kyle was obviously to *not* be in direct sales forever, standing in a department store for long hours each day selling television service never actually ended. It only increased, along with a slew of other responsibilities.

While the umbrella of labor laws protected his employees from long hours, it certainly didn't protect him as the business owner. He was left to pick up the slack at every turn. The money may have made it all worthwhile, *had there been any*. But the money coming in was not enough to cover the money going out.

In addition to office rent, ads, recruiting, payroll, insurance, and supplies, he was also encouraged – *ahem, coerced* – by the organization into footing the bill on regular team outings and constant business trips to see what other markets were doing "right" and where he was going "wrong". He was always expected to take a few employees along with him on these trips to experience what a bigger office was like, in order to inspire and motivate them. As you can imagine, the cost of these things added up quickly.

We were engaged when Kyle moved to start up his office. Once we were married, I moved to live with him, my job agreeing to let me work remotely. As newlyweds, we rented a home not just with each other, but also with his assistant manager and, at that point, another employee as well that he had hired from his promoting office back home.

I also got to know his other employees well. In an attempt to help the business look more professional, I set up my remote desk in the front lobby of his office, as though I were his receptionist. He needed someone to greet the candidates coming in for interviews and provide them with the paperwork they needed to fill out. It was an obvious choice for me to do this for him, as it took up very little of my time and got me out of the house while saving him the money required to hire someone. So, as the first person that people met that helped them with their new hire paperwork, who answered many of their questions, collected their timecards, and approved their time off requests, I ended up having a relationship with everyone that came into the business.

On top of that, I was privy to all of the morning meetings and all of the weekly owner's calls. I attended all of the company outings and even went on the company business trips since I could work from anywhere. Slowly, but surely, I began taking on more and more responsibilities. So, when Kyle asked me to quit my job and officially take on the role of office manager and recruiter for the company, I obliged.

One would think that this would have been a difficult decision for me, seeing as how I was making good money and had great benefits at my job, while Kyle wasn't making a dime, and going more and more into debt each week. My job, after all, was the only thing keeping us afloat.

But it wasn't a difficult decision at all. I had been exposed to the organization's messaging and jargon for so long, that I had begun buying into the rhetoric and all of the hype. My "cushy" 9-5 job, as they called it, was constantly being belittled – not mine specifically or directly, but as an overall consensus that entrepreneurs were superior to those settling into the long-term role of employee – "employee" being a dirty word within the company.

Everyone in the organization was working their butt off to pursue the American Dream, to achieve what they considered greatness while working for someone else was considered to be taking the easy road. All anyone ever did was talk about how great of an opportunity they had been given. So, when I too, had the opportunity to go all-in right along with Kyle, I did. I drank the Kool-Aid.

Our debt continued to compound. That financial pressure, along with trying to work together, yet hardly ever seeing each other outside of the office and at team events, and having little to no privacy since we lived with two of his male employees during our first year of marriage, was a strain, *to say the least*.

Fast forward a year and a half later. We found ourselves both mentally and physically exhausted and on the brink of a mental breakdown. Kyle was still working seven days a week, extremely long hours, and I was living completely out of alignment in my role as a recruiter for a company I no longer believed in.

I had begun to realize that the promises we were making to our employees, and the ones I was making over the phone to candidates trying to entice them to come in for an interview, were not real. And while my anxiety over this made it physically difficult for me to pick up the phone every morning, much less look our employees in the eye, the much larger anxiety I felt over *failing my husband* kept me doing it.

My numbers (as in interviews scheduled each day) were being reviewed by the organization just as much as his sales numbers were. The ultimate reality was, if I couldn't keep the constant revolving door of candidates coming in, Kyle didn't stand a chance of working any less or making any more money. He could lose his contract with the stores, and thus, lose his business. Everyone was relying on me, including his employees, who also didn't stand a chance of moving up if they didn't have anyone to mentor, as they had to grow a team in order to be promoted.

This was the only marketing involved in our marketing company – the marketing of the "opportunity" itself, which was required to hire new sales reps on a consistent basis. There was constant pressure from multiple directions to do better, to *be* better. I was not just letting Kyle down if I failed, but his entire team. This was, indeed, the only way to make the business a success. If I failed in my role as his recruiter, the business failed too.

While I had excelled at the job in the beginning when I believed in what I was telling people, my words had become hollow shells, as my thoughts and beliefs were no longer in alignment with my actions, and people could feel it. I got more and more into my head and became less and less effective as time went on. While I no longer wanted to be in that position, essentially lying to people every single day, I couldn't fathom telling that to Kyle, knowing that it would put all of the work and stress back on his shoulders. I also just didn't think he would understand. He lived and breathed the business. If I came to him with my concerns, I figured he would just think that I couldn't hack it, that I wasn't made for the pressure, that I was giving up.

And so, due to what I now realize was cult-like behavior in an organization with a particularly charismatic team of leaders, I kept quiet and trudged ahead, holding our united front. I continued on pretending as though being an owner was as glamorous as it was made out to be, and encouraging others to keep working for us. We spent money like we had it, pretended to be happy when we were anything but, and kept up the façade that all was great in the land of ownership – the treasure was worth it.

It wasn't until I missed the birth of my niece, Kylie, that it began to sink in how much we had become prisoners to the organization. We had been separated from our family and friends, our only friends now our employees, and were kept working around the clock so that we had no time to visit or hardly even have a phone conversation with anyone outside of the organization. As a matter of fact, we were expected to have one-on-one phone calls each week with people *inside* the organization, leaving no room for the former. We were exhausted, as it was a 24-hour gig that seemed to never end.

Anytime an owner did try to take a step back or take a break, the higher-ups in the organization would be all over them immediately, constantly calling people out on the weekly owner calls and threatening those not working hard enough with a re-train, which meant you'd again have to spend your own money to go to another office to relearn the rules of success.

We had been brainwashed. We heard the same messages over and over again from people we trusted and admired. They played on our hopes and dreams, and our weaknesses. The problem was, once we realized what was going on, we were in too deep. We'd made promises to people we cared about, people that we now considered family, and we were deeply in debt, both personally and to the organization.

It was easier to just keep believing. So, we continued to believe them when they said it would get better, that it would all eventually pay off. We believed them when they said we needed to just work a little harder. We believed them when they said that new clients and products were being on-boarded so that we'd have more to sell than just television service. We believed them when they said that bigger markets were coming and that we were next in line to move up. We believed them when they said that outside deals were coming for our employees that were ready to be promoted to owners themselves, and that the overrides we would receive from these promotions would make it all worthwhile.

But it was all a lie. New products, bigger markets, and outside deals weren't coming. All of the big cities had offices already, and those owners weren't going anywhere. The offices in big cities, much like the one Kyle was promoted out of, were the organization's bread and butter. Due to the larger populations, new sales were easily generated, but that wasn't where the real money was – it was in the revolving door of candidates that were able to be brought in, which led to the new owners they were able to promote, and the outrageous fees they were then able to collect from those owners. When it was time to promote someone to an outside deal, it was the big cities that were the ones to get those "opportunities", not the smaller offices.

The smaller offices were left to squander and starve until they had no choice but to give up. *These* were the new territories coming available – just completely saturated markets with a long line of failed owners that never stood a chance of making it. And when they inevitably did fail, then guess what? Their failure meant another new outside deal for a big city office. Another promotion, another celebration, more motivation for the employees working toward ownership as they saw people getting promoted out left and right, assuming it would be the same for them once they were ready, too. Turnover was the name of the game, new excitement, fresh faces, oblivious to what was going on.

The only thing that kept the organization classified as a multi-level marketing company, rather than an illegal pyramid scheme, was that the "buy in" was cleverly disguised as normal business ownership costs. But when the recruiter and payroll provider are in-house, charging far more than any typical recruiting or payroll company would, and you pay so much in fees to your promoting company and parent organization, that the only way you can make a profit is to recruit and train new owners, it gets more than a little dicey in the distinction between the two.

The organization kept owners pot-committed, in a sort of all-in mentality. They kept them in debt, in the dark, and shamed them into investing what little money they made back into their employees and back into the business. Once in that position, you want to believe their promises even more, because you see no other way to dig yourself out of the hole you are in.

Owners worked around the clock, not even making minimum wage. This is how the organization thrived. Not just cheap labor, but *free* labor, labor with ridiculously high fees paid by the laborers. And labor performed as though the laborer's life depended on it. Our livelihood was threatened to be taken away at any moment if we stopped to catch our breath. Of course that was a no-no, perhaps they understood a thing or two about intuition.

It became obvious that the organization preyed on inexperienced, naive recent graduates who had never been in the workforce before and had nothing to compare their experience to. As we were following their rules, we now *were* the "organization" – i.e. the ones doing the preying.

During my training to become a recruiter, I was told to look for recent graduates because younger people had more energy, more enthusiasm, more dedication. I quickly realized it was actually because younger people were just more gullible, more excitable. They didn't ask as many questions. They were hungry for a job, any job, especially one that had the opportunity of making big money. The older people that I talked to just wouldn't take the bait. They wanted to know exactly what it was they would be doing each day and in each phase of the training model. Even if my lies got them in for an interview, once they saw how young everyone was, including the owner, they knew something was off.

From the first recruiting phone call making promises about a creative job in marketing campaigns, event planning, and relationship building with Fortune 500 clients, to the money owners pretended to be stacking away, the deeper and deeper we got into it, the more we realized it was all smoke and mirrors. It didn't matter how far up the chain we went, behind each curtain was one Wizard of Oz after another. The best of the best owners in the best markets, who were propped up on pedestals by the organization, their egos being fed constantly, were heavily brainwashed into thinking they were the epitome of success, while still *living* with their own employees, trying to make ends meet. And this was who we were aspiring to be?

We had put our faith in the wrong people, blindly following them based on promises that were not real. Deep down inside we knew it much earlier than we consciously realized, but we had allowed external forces to make us question, if not completely block out, our faith within – our own intuition. And the disconnect between our knowing and our being had made us both sick.

I was living with strangers, my husband working around the clock, in a city where we had no family or friends other than our own employees, employees that I could now barely look in the eye, and missing out on everything that was important to me. I was filled with anxiety that continued to compound day after day, until I found myself trying to dig my way out of a very lonely and deep, dark hole of depression. I felt stuck, with nowhere to go and no one to turn to.

I came home one day to find Kyle lying on the couch in the middle of the afternoon with tears in his eyes. He was never home in the middle of the day, so I knew something very bad had happened.

He shared with me that he had been to the doctor, who had prescribed him medication for anxiety and depression. My husband, Mr. Optimistic himself, depressed, as well? It was then that I let the floodgates open and told him everything that I felt too – everything I'd observed, questioned, and no longer believed.

Afterward, we looked at each other, relieved. Once we had said it all out loud, there was no denying it. We finally, consciously knew that this thing we had been a part of wasn't right.

We knew it was time to cut our losses and get out of an increasingly bad situation. Our egoic minds tried to interfere. I remember even saying out loud at one point, "Maybe we should just work a couple more weeks, build up a little money in the bank, before we close it all down." We had nothing, after all, no money to even fund the already owed payroll the following week, as we'd been working on a week-to-week basis. We also had nothing to help us get back on our feet – to pay for moving costs, or a deposit on a new place back home, or even to pay for our most basic needs, like food, in the interim.

And honestly, I was terrified. I wasn't just scared for our livelihood, I was scared of the organization itself – of what kind of legal repercussions there might be in that contract Kyle had signed so hastily when he opened his business, that he wasn't even given a copy of. We felt like we were fleeing a cult in the middle of the night, sure that they would get in our way and try to stop us by any means necessary.

But Kyle refused to let it go on any longer, he was done being taken advantage of, and now that he knew how I felt about it as well, it was the motivation he needed to get us out. He immediately fired all of the employees, sharing what we had learned with those that had been in it with us for the long haul, and closed down the business. We had nothing to show for all of our hard work, just two unemployed, very soon-to-be homeless people, with a mountain of debt to boot.

That moment could have been the end of Kyle's big dreams. It was, after all, a *massive* failure. But somewhere deep down in his heart, he still believed that he would have the freedom one day that he'd always desired. *Real* freedom, not the fake promise of freedom that had kept him feeling enslaved, doing things he did not want to do, while being sold the illusion of choice.

We moved back home and I was fortunate to get my old job back, still working remotely, so that we could move closer to our families this time, which I was happy about. Kyle got a mindless, manual labor job over the next few months, which was exactly the reprieve he needed from the mental exhaustion he had been grappling with. We struggled to make ends meet for the next year, trying to dig ourselves out of the hole of debt we'd created.

One good thing about multi-level marketing companies, *and some cults* unfortunately, is that they focus heavily on mindset and personal development. It is intoxicating – this idea that your limitations are self-imposed, that you are capable of far more than you had previously believed, that you can become a better version of yourself, and change your entire life. They teach you how to always be learning and growing, and give you the tools to master yourself.

This is how they draw people in and why they are so magnetic. Because in the beginning, they *do* speak the truth, and those hearing it know deep down in their soul, that it's real, that they really do have far more power than they'd given themselves credit for. And for many, it's the first time they've heard such truths, the first time they are able to truly believe in themselves.

Of course, these organizations then use the trust they've gained for their own purposes, sometimes evil purposes, and convince you that whatever it is that they are offering is the *only* means for success. But far before this is revealed, they've opened your mind to the energetic power of your thoughts, beliefs, and actions.

It may have been that this path that we had been set on was the very reason that I had delved so heavily into personal development and had found the book *The Secret*, which prompted me to put my first vision board together. That focus is what had inspired me to begin making changes in our lives. It's what led to my promotion at work and to acquiring a second job, as well as Kyle's next job in logistics.

It had been easy to convince Kyle to get back into the business world. After a year of breaking his back, doing manual labor for cheap pay, he was more than ready. I helped him get his resume together and apply for jobs. He ended up accepting an entry-level position at a global logistics firm.

He learned fast, and quickly became a successful broker. But even though he was brokering huge deals, the commission he was receiving was not reflecting it. He also couldn't help but notice the commonalities between his new job and his last experience.

The logistics firm recruited kids right out of school and treated them like a number, paying them a draw on their commission and ready to fire them at any opportunity for not following by their rules, which seemed to be designed to make them fail. Once fired, that person's clients were quickly handed over to someone else in the company who deserved the upper hand based on their hard work. There were big celebrations for big wins for the employees based on an aggressive training and promotion model, but while the night of drinking in your honor was fun, the company was the one who reaped all of the monetary rewards of the broker's hard work, *not* the broker themselves.

There were too many red flags for Kyle after all that he'd been through, and he simply didn't believe it. He made a deal with one of his customers to go to work for them. This time it was with a well-known commodities dealer that had started up a logistics division. His job would be to help get the local office up and running successfully. And he did just that.

Kyle's first year was to be focused on operations rather than sales since he had a non-compete agreement that would be in effect. After that, they would hire someone else to handle operations and he could get back to doing what he did best.

This unfortunately never came to be, and although a high-paying commission structure was a big part of his salary negotiations when he accepted the position, the commission structure was impossible to understand, and he rarely ever received a commission payment. For two years he fought with the higher-ups, trying to get accurate reporting and to get paid for the work he was doing. Once again, it all felt far too familiar.

After a particularly frustrating call with his boss where he was given the run-around once again, he decided if he wasn't going to receive commission as promised, he was going to ask for a raise in his base pay. He asked for a small $5,000-a-year raise for the work he had done over the previous two years to grow the company. We spent over two hours drafting an email outlining all of his accomplishments and responsibilities.

The raise was quickly denied. In that moment, Kyle snapped. He decided he was done working for people that took advantage of him. He decided the only way to get paid fairly for all the work he put in was to go out on his own and start his own business. *Again.*

Except *this* time, he was doing it based solely on his faith in *himself*, not on anyone else's promises. And *this* time, he was going after *real* freedom. Not just financial freedom, which had been his goal at all three of his prior jobs, but full freedom of autonomy over every area of his life, which he had learned was just as important as the money.

It was November 2019, just a month before Christmas, and we had yet to buy presents based on the fact that we were still in the hole financially. Kyle's boss had promised he would receive a Christmas bonus and we had been banking on that in order to afford gifts. Once again, I asked him if we could wait. If we could at least wait until after that bonus, until after Christmas, when conditions were a little better. How would we make ends meet while he got up and running with just my paycheck alone? And what if they came after him due to the non-compete agreement that he had signed with them? I was scared, yet again.

But just as Khloe's eyes had told a story when she was trying to take her first steps, the resolve in Kyle's eyes was unwavering. He told me that he would be careful, he wouldn't touch any of their customers or carriers and would give them no reason to come after him. But even if they did, he assured me it would be better than continuing to work for them. He couldn't believe that a Christmas bonus was even coming, regardless of what they had said, because they'd proved themselves to be liars and he couldn't continue working for them knowing this. He was done, and it was time to act *now*. He looked me in the eye and told me that *he would not fail.* And I believed him.

He quit his job and over the next few weeks, started up an LLC. Due to the non-compete agreement, he was forced to start over completely, which wasn't easy touting a business name no one had ever heard of. But even when there was no paycheck week after week and nothing to show for all of his hard work, he refused to give up. He refused to accept failure and held on firmly to his belief in himself.

That belief was tested many times during his first year in business, even after he started signing on clients. Just as he had started to get rolling, the Covid-19 pandemic struck, shutting down businesses all over the country. And then, as if that wasn't enough to deter his progress, our lives were completely uprooted at the end of 2020 after my sister's accident, taking so much of our time and focus away from the business.

But Kyle put his head down and continued to put one foot in front of the other, taking the actions that he knew were right, fighting through all of the fear, and failure, and hardships, and refusing to accept defeat. He forged ahead, all the while believing that his success was inevitable, all the while speaking *only* of that inevitable success.

Despite a particularly rough start, his first full year in business he ended up doing over $300k in revenue and personally profiting a little over $80k before taxes. In his second year, he did over $1.1 million in revenue and profited around $300k. Now, in his third year, he is set to double what he did prior, making it a multi-million-dollar business and making us a net-profit of over a million dollars.

He quantum leaped.

As Steve Jobs once said, "You cannot connect the dots looking forward; You can only connect them looking backwards. So, you have to trust that the dots will somehow connect in your future." I'd like to add to this, *in your favor.* Looking back now, it is easy to see how all the pieces fell together just perfectly for Kyle's big dreams to come true, even though it certainly didn't seem that way in the years leading up to it. But those years, each and every failure, were actually *crucial* to his inevitable success.

Kyle never made a *wrong* step. He followed his intuition and it brought him every step of the way along a journey that taught him exactly what he needed to learn to get to where he needed to be. And while it had felt like one set back after another, it was actually just a windy road to success. It was as though the Universe provided him with all of the hard lessons that he needed in order to become who he dreamed of becoming, in the shortest time possible.

His first failed business venture with the marketing company was exactly what he needed at the time, a hundred lessons all rolled into one. What he learned during that massive failure was invaluable. He had learned how to become a killer at sales – how to take at least a hundred no's a day, and still power through to get the one yes. He'd learned how to lead, inspire, and motivate others, and how to manage multiple employees. He had learned how to start up and run his own business. Together, we had learned how to follow that feeling in our gut, and to speak up when something didn't sit right. We'd also learned, through much trial and tribulation, how to work together, and how to rely on each other's strengths, while picking up the slack for each other's weaknesses. We learned that together, we were far more powerful than we were on our own. This would prove to be exponentially important down the road.

Perhaps most importantly, Kyle got a very clear picture of everything he *didn't* want as a business owner. He didn't want shady behind-the-scenes activity, but rather clear transparency for everyone involved in his business. He didn't want to have his hands tied on how he treated his own employees, but wanted to be able to give them time off anytime he pleased, pay them what they deserved, and give bonuses and raises based on their hard work, not just based on results. He realized how important independence and freedom were to him – how important the freedom over his own money, time, values, and personal choices were, and he wanted to be able to give that to the people that worked for him as well.

Though he didn't make much money in his first job in logistics and therefore could call that a failure as well, he got trained by one of the best logistics companies in the world. He got a taste for the industry and fell in love with it. The hustle and grind were different than it had been selling television service to shoppers. It was still hard work, but the kind of work that was interesting to him, that always kept him on his toes and kept him learning, that actually did thrive on relationship building and creative thinking. And, seeing first hand, such high profit margins for the company, he saw the potential for what kind of money could be made if one were in charge of their own destiny, which motivated him more than anything in his life had ever done before.

His failure at the second logistics company, where he had put his blood, sweat, and tears into getting off the ground, was also devastating to him at the time. But again, it was *exactly* what he needed, and had set him up for his eventual success. He had learned how to manage multi-million-dollar accounts and had formed relationships and made connections that would pay off exponentially later on down the road, once his non-compete agreement was up.

Most importantly, he'd gotten the slap in the face that he needed, one that stung so deeply it gave him no other choice but to say "no more," and to truly mean it, just as I truly meant it when I decided my job was my last priority. Getting that fed up was what forced him to start over on his own, something that he may have never done if he had been making a comfortable, decent salary at the firm. The disregard for his hard work and expertise was so blatant that it also gave *me* what *I* needed to support him in taking another ride on the entrepreneurial train while we were still in debt from the first one.

One failure after another led him down this path, a path in which all of his dreams ended up coming true. Many times, Kyle could have accepted failure and given up. He could have given up on his dreams of being an entrepreneur after his first failed business venture, or when our debt kept us tied to our weekly paychecks. He could have given up on being a logistics broker when a non-compete agreement took away his livelihood and he had to start over from scratch. He could have given up on his now multi-million-dollar business when he heard "no" for the one-hundredth time while cold calling, or when he didn't receive a paycheck for the 12th week in a row.

But he didn't give up. He held faith in the vision within him, took action based on that calling, and made the decision to leap, time and time again, when it felt like the right thing to do. He leaped even when it was scary to do so, even when there was no net to catch him if he fell, even after he *did* fall. And because of that, *he flew.*

> *"The moment you doubt whether you can fly, you cease*
> *forever to be able to do it."*

PETER PAN

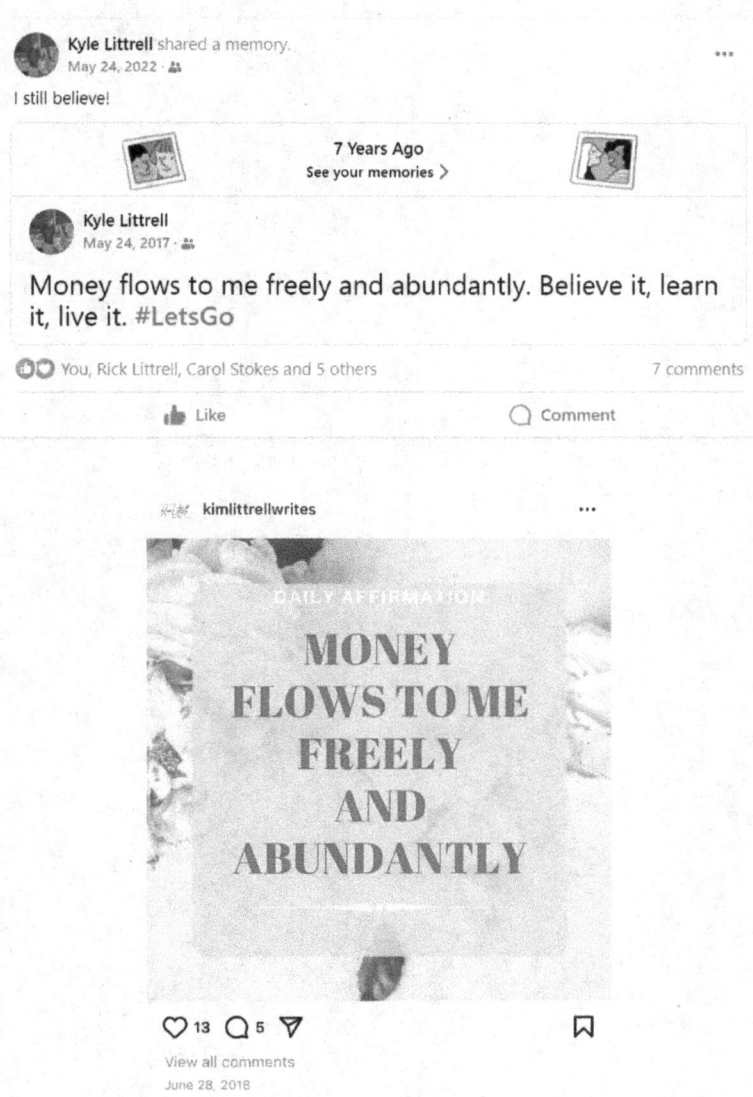

Believe it to See It (Kyle and Kim's Posts from 2017 & 2018)

LESSONS ON FREEDOM

*"Things that matter most must never be at the mercy of
things that matter least."*

JOHANN WOLFGANG VON GOETHE

Be, Do, Have to Quantum Leap

"First say to yourself what you will *be*; and then *do* what you have to do." –
Epictetus, first century Stoic philosopher.

If you want to reverse-engineer success, what you must first understand is
that it is not about what you accomplish. It is about who you *become* in the
process. And when you come at it from this angle of understanding, you know
it is not about what you *do*, it is about who you *be*.

When most people think about their dream life, they tend to think about
obtaining it in the following order of: *Have, Do, Be.* As in, "When I *have* this, I
will *do* this, and then I will *be* this."

An example of this was my old way of thinking, "When I *have* the time, I
will *write* the book, and then I will *be* a best-selling author." The problem with
this common way of thinking is that it is backward, and it will rarely ever lead
to becoming who you want to be. It places a focus on having something
external, outside of yourself – in my case, *time* – before being able to take action
to do what you want to do and be who you want to be.

Another example could be: "When I *have* the money to invest in it, I will
then *do* the learning program, and then I will *be* a world-famous designer."
Again, you are waiting on something external, *money*, as if it is outside of your
control, to come to you before taking action to do what you want to do and be
who you want to be.

If you follow this method of thinking, you will spend your entire life waiting

105

and then regretting *all* of that time that you spent waiting. Waiting for perfect conditions to begin will keep you from realizing your dreams 100% of the time, because conditions will *never* be perfect.

If Kyle would have waited for better conditions to shut down his first failed business, perhaps until we had a little bit of money saved up in the bank, or had secured another job, he could still be there today, still waiting, or possibly drawn back in. If he'd waited to quit his job and start the logistics company until after Christmas, or after we'd gotten out of debt, he may have never done it. It could have taken us *years* to get out of debt had we not made such a massive change. But he didn't wait. He struck when the iron was hot, when it felt like the right thing to do in every bone of his body, *regardless* of external conditions and what we did, or did not, have.

If you are making excuses now, like a snowball effect they will only compound and grow heavier. As time goes on, your life will only become more convoluted and complicated and you will come up with more and more excuses.

People often put off having children even though they want them, until they are in a better place financially, have a bigger home, live in a better school district, or work at a less stressful job. The list could go on and on. But as most parents will tell you, once you have a child, you simply make it work. The tools, knowledge, and the resources come. Everything in life is just like this.

If you want to make your dreams a reality, you must stop waiting on external factors to change before taking action. To accomplish your dreams, you must learn to start with the *being*, now, well before you actually are, and then take action from that place of being.

You have likely heard the phrase "Fake it until you make it" or "Act as if…", which is associated with the Law of Assumption, a spiritual belief that whatever you assume to be true becomes your reality. If you've ever followed the advice to smile when you are sad to turn your mood around, then you've experienced this first hand. You likely saw how taking the action to smile resulted in feeling better much quicker than had you waited on something external to change your mood and *make* you smile.

The action of smiling signals to your brain and body that there is a *reason* to smile – something positive or enjoyable *must* be happening. Even a forced smile can trigger physiological and psychological responses that contribute to a more positive mood.

Of course, there are scientific reasons for this. Smiling releases endorphins and dopamine, which are neurotransmitters that reduce stress and pain, lower cortisol, and act as natural mood lifters, contributing to feelings of pleasure and relaxation – which thus, give you *reasons* to smile.

Not only does your mind and body respond to your actions, but your external reality does as well. When you smile, it positively impacts social interactions, leading to increased feelings of connection and support. Your smile elicits smiles from others and this in turn shifts their mood as well, which can often result in more favorable outcomes in your interactions. Again, now you have reasons to smile.

So, by choosing to take the action to smile before you have a reason to smile, your reality responds to you and eventually aligns with the action you are taking as though you already are happy. You are given more and more reasons to smile. Your smile creates a vibration within you, and outside of you, and soon your external reality calibrates to your internal state of being.

The key to success is not just focusing on what you want as in section one, or believing in it as in section two, but also in taking the action steps to *be* who you need to be in order to accomplish what you want to accomplish, and doing so *before* you are "ready."

The secret is that you are never ready until you actually take that first step. This is how you *become* ready – by taking one step and then another, and doing it again and again, no matter how scary it is, or how many times you fail. Do the things now that you would do if you already were who you wanted to be. Just as I contacted a realtor and we started telling people we were buying a house before we were actually ready to do so, take the steps now that you would take if you already had the means or the resources you need, before you actually have them. Act "as if" and the resources will inevitably fall into place.

Everything you need to accomplish your dreams is a potential in the quantum field around you. Remember that potentials are endless. If you want to pick out a particular energetic potential, then you must become a vibrational match to it, you must get into alignment with it. You do this not just with your thoughts, not just with your beliefs, but also with your actions. When these three things align – your thoughts, your beliefs, and your actions – energy moves.

If you were to study the most successful people in the world, you would find that, certainly early on, but likely many times throughout their lives, they all took a leap of faith, even when there was no net to catch them if they fell.

You often hear the age-old story of the actor or actress who moved to Hollywood with $20 in their pocket. No net. This was not them *doing* before they were *being*, although it certainly appears that way on the surface. Internally, they already were *being* – they *already were* the famous actor in their *mind* – before the *doing* – before packing up their car and driving to Hollywood. If they weren't already "acting as if", or assuming the identity of the person that could do the thing, they would never have the courage to make the leap. Their internal belief became reality when they took action that aligned with that belief – this is what shifted their external reality.

Of course, one can still expect to experience failures while they are getting into alignment and strengthening their beliefs through physical action, but that failure is *how* you learn, how you gain the critical information and experience needed to become the you that you desire to be.

Just as Khloe did when learning to walk, if you keep stepping out into the unknown, you, too, will eventually do what you have set out to do. We certainly don't look at babies who try, and fail to walk, and think, *well this one just doesn't have what it takes*. Just because you fail does not mean you do not have what it takes. It simply means you need to *build up* what it takes, and you do this through action. This is how humans learn. They try, they fail, they reassess, they revise their methods, and they try again. And eventually, one of their revised methods brings about success.

Don't take it from me, take a look at Michael Jordan who was cut from his high school varsity team, only to later become the best basketball player of all time. In the words of a fellow basketball star, Kobe Bryant, "Obsession beats talent." I would venture to add to this statement, *every single time in the long-run*. Jordan may have lacked natural talent, but he was obsessed with basketball, so giving up was not an option, no matter how much he failed. In his own words, "I've missed more than 9,000 shots in my career. I've lost almost 300 games. Twenty-six times, I've been trusted to take the game winning shot and missed. I've failed over and over and over again in my life. And that is why I succeed."

According to Kanters Law, everything looks like a failure in the middle. It is this perception of failure on one's way to success that makes people sabotage their own efforts. You must reframe your thoughts around failure if you want to succeed. You must see it as a stepping stone, one step closer, rather than a step backward or worse, the end of the road.

You must refuse to give up. You must be willing to be bad at something new in order to get good at it. You must take chances and go all in, even when you don't have the resources or the skills to back it up.

Eventually, the skills and the resources will come. The net will appear. This is how you take massive quantum leaps forward in your life, by *being* the you that already is who you want to be, and doing the things you would do if you already were, *even* before you are ready.

Ask yourself, if I already was who I wanted to be, what would that version of me do now? Act as if your success is not only inevitable, but as if it is already done, and make the leap as though it is.

Where would a famous actor or actress live? Hollywood, exactly. What would a best-selling author do? They would write every single morning. They would begin talking about their work. They would pay for a developmental edit to get things moving in the right direction. What would the millionaire business owner do? They wouldn't wait another second to establish the LLC. They would hire before they are "ready" in anticipation for what is coming. They would find a financial advisor even if they hadn't yet made a penny.

What would that version of you do that already is who you want to be? What would you do if your success were inevitable? If it was all already on its way to you, what would be your next step?

A good way to think about this is to engage in child's play. As a child, you inherently knew that all you had to *do* was *be*. When you dreamed of being a teacher, you didn't wait until you grew up, went to school, got a degree, and then got a job, to start teaching. You started teaching in the *now*, in the very moment you thought of it, right where you were, with what you had.

Sure, the imaginary classroom was made up of imaginary children and you weren't an expert in the subject matter at hand, but you didn't care. You simply *acted* as if you were a teacher, because you wanted to *be* a teacher. And through this play, this "practice" if you will, you likely got pretty damn good at being a teacher. At first, you were unprepared, you floundered and made mistakes, you ran out of things to say, but eventually, you held class and it was perfect. All of the practice paid off.

You may have even gotten so good at being a teacher that you started believing you really *could* be a teacher. You may have eventually gone to school, got a degree, got a job, and *became* a teacher.

There is magic in the willingness to put yourself out there and to begin. It is all about being willing to start wherever you are, with whatever you have, or *don't* have, even if it feels like make-believe. Keep pretending – this is how you collapse time and quantum leap into your dream life.

There is no external thing outside of yourself that you must have to do what you want to do. You must simply make the decision that it is your priority, decide to start *being* that version of yourself, and then take action as though you already are, putting one foot in front of the other to take each next step *before* you feel as though you are ready.

The Lie of Tomorrow

People often get stuck in the planning phase of their dreams, thinking that if they can just plan out every single detail before they get started, *then* they will be ready. *Then* everything will go smoothly. But as one of my favorite books, *Of Mice and Men* declares, "The best laid plans of mice and men often go astray."

The problem is that you don't *know* every single detail that needs to be planned, every single step that needs to be taken, until you are there, until you are in it. You have no idea what is to come after you take that first step. You just have to take each step to find out.

Will taking the first step lead to accomplishing your dreams? Maybe, maybe not. You may find along the way that what you thought you wanted isn't actually what you want after all. You may find somewhere down the path something else that excites you even more. Or you may find that you never waiver in your desire for this one thing and you end up accomplishing exactly what you set out to accomplish. Regardless of the outcome, if you never begin, you will never know. That dream will stay stuck in your head. You will never accomplish it and you will never move on from it. You will never dream any bigger.

When you are young, life can seem monotonous and never-ending, as if it will span on forever. What you do today, in this moment, can seem irrelevant in the grand scheme of things. After all, there is always another tomorrow. You can start eating healthy or meditating or working out...*tomorrow*. You can start drawing or painting or writing, creating, or building or designing...*tomorrow*. You can research or network or practice...*tomorrow*. You can show up, stand up for yourself, or tell that special someone how you feel...*tomorrow*.

We often put off the things that we really want out of life because we feel overwhelmed by the commitment, dedication, and time that will be required of us to see it through. We feel overwhelmed with the high chance of failure, of the high chance of embarrassment. So rather than getting started, we choose to tell ourselves a lie. We tell ourselves that someday in the future, the time, the motivation, the resources, or the perfect conditions will magically appear. We tell ourselves that someday we will follow through on our dreams, that somehow, we will be different than we are today.

When you approach your life in this way, you will inevitably find yourself the victim of a time warp. While the days will often seem long, the years will be short, and time will pass quicker than you could ever imagine. A tired, old man (or woman) filled with regrets will stare back at you in the mirror where a vibrant kid with dreams once stood. You will wonder where the time went and why you wished away all of your todays on tomorrows that never came.

Regardless of what you do or don't do today, the time will pass – that you can be sure of. One day you will turn around and you will be five, ten, twenty years older than you are today. So, the question need not ever be how much time something will take to accomplish, because the time will pass anyway, but rather, who do you want to be in one, five, ten, or twenty years?

Do you want to be the same you, just a little more wrinkled and grey, with all the same dreams stuck in your head that you were never brave enough to pursue? Wondering if you could have achieved them by now had you started back then? Do you want to be the you that's living a life full of regret, always wondering *what if? What if I had actually gone all in? What if I had taken that first step?*

Or, do you want to be the you that you always dreamed of becoming, or possibly even something greater? The you that pulled those dreams out of your head and put in the work back then to make them your reality now? The you that is happy, and fulfilled, and proud, living out your dream life, and working on even bigger and brighter dreams?

Both of those *you's* are a potential in the quantum field. All you need to do is match the vibration of the *you* that you desire. Hold the vision of the *you* that you want to become and then move like her, talk like her, take steps toward her – not tomorrow, but *today*.

Who you are and who you become can only be determined in the fluidity and moldability of the omni-powerful, ever-present now. The now, this moment, is all there ever really is. Everything else, the past and the future, is just a figment of your imagination – a simple story you have told yourself.

Your life is made up of the compound effect of a series of *nows*. And to change your life, all you have to do is change the *now*. You are always just one decision away from a completely different life.

The simple decision to begin is so often what separates the ordinary from the extraordinary. Most people never begin. If you want to be extraordinary, make the decision to begin, and begin *now*. Not tomorrow, but *now*. And then build on that action every single day as you draw the potential reality of what you desire toward you.

An entirely new timeline will unfold before you, one in which your dreams have already manifested. And you'll look back down that timeline, sooner than you could have ever imagined, and think: *That was the moment. That first step is what changed everything.*

The first step creates momentum in the direction of your dreams just as potently as not taking that first step creates momentum in the opposite direction of your dreams. You are always moving toward your desires or moving away from them, but you *are* always moving. Do not convince yourself that not taking that first step is simply staying where you are, because it's not. The entire Universe is moving, the Earth is spinning, and you are changing. You are always gaining momentum in one direction or another, plundering ahead along the timeline of your choosing.

Rather than allowing yourself to become the victim of a time warp, you can choose to collapse time in your favor by being who you want to be *now*, in this very moment. Then, sit back and watch in awe as the entire Universe shifts to align with the frequency of your being. This is how you take back your power and control over time, and make massive quantum leaps forward in your life.

The Greatest Illusion of Man

"Time and space are not conditions in which we live, but modes by which we think. Physical concepts are free creations of the human mind, and are not, however it may seem, determined by the external world...Time does not exist – we invented it. Time is what the clock says. The distinction between the past, present, and future is only a stubbornly persistent illusion," Albert Einstein.

Much like everything else in our world, the concept of time is man, or more specifically, *mind*-made. It is a carefully built illusion. The time is now and the now is eternal, for the past was *once* the now, the present is *certainly* the now, and the future will *someday be* the now. It is always only now. If now is actually all that there ever really is, and it is eternal, time therefore, as we have been led to understand it, does not really exist.

Time may be a carefully crafted illusion, but it still plays a defining role in the way we perceive reality. The meaning we assign to time has the ability to create either a sense of freedom in our lives, or a sense of enslavement, depending on how much power we choose to give it. Unfortunately for most people, it is the latter – they are *enslaved* to time. Afterall, if you don't *have* time, then apparently time *has you*.

If you were to dig into the concept of time, you would find that traditionally accepted beliefs and collective phrases such as time *spent*, time *wasted*, and time *lost* have become our norm. There is hardly ever any mention of an *abundance* of time, for we have made the *lack* of time very real to us.

This lack of time mentality is one of the greatest illusions of man. It is an illusion that has been nailed tightly into place by society and accepted by the masses as truth. With every tick, of every minute, on every clock, with every year, and every birthday that passes, this concept is reinforced and engrained deeper into our minds, and thus, our realities.

Our entire lives revolve around a clock, a clock that was imagined, and is orchestrated, by someone else entirely. Yet, we collectively accept this concept of time, this circular device with its hands constantly moving, as our own. We adhere to it as if it is the ultimate truth, allowing it to dictate every part of our lives.

Our days begin and end based on this clock. We have appropriate times for sleeping and waking, for learning or working, for meals and breaks, and for appointments and meetings. We have established weekdays and weekends, often an allotment of personal time, vacation time, and sick time. And on a grander scale, we have collectively acceptable time ranges for learning and development, for career exploration and growth, for marriage and childbirth, for retirement, for travel and play, and even for rest.

This clock, which lends to the calendar, is such a staple in our lives that we look to it for permission at every thought or idea that enters our mind. We stomp out the urgings of our intuition in favor of societal norms and constructs that demand our allegiance.

Many of us spend our entire lives fighting against this clock, to no avail. We rush around day after day, late for this or that, in a self-defeating, pointless pursuit, adhering to everyone else's expectations of us, expectations that require more time than we feel we have to give. The clock keeps moving, the days and years keep passing, and we spend our time desperately trying to keep up, all the while believing that we've never done enough to get ahead, and constantly wishing for more time to do the things we actually *want* to do.

We have created a reality for ourselves in which there is *never enough time*. But what is there Never Enough Time *for*? I like to think of this as NET time. The amount of time left to do the things you *truly* want to do: To pursue joy, to pursue your heart's desires, dreams, passions, and purpose. There never seems to be enough time for these once you have removed all of the other time spent on the trivial day-to-day demands of you.

So how does one create more time to do the things they actually want to do with their life? How does one go from NET (Never Enough Time), to an *abundance* of time?

First, you must be reminded of Einstein's theory of relativity. Just as its name implies, it proves that time is relative to the observer. Two people can perceive and experience time differently based on their frame of reference. $E=mc2$, which we touched on at the beginning of this book, is the equation used to explain relativity. What does this tell you? Once again, we come back to the conclusion that *everything is energy*. And energy is what creates matter. Those ticking hands on your clock *are* energy and are *affected by* energy, in the same way that everything else in the Universe is.

The ancient Greeks had two different words to describe two very different experiences regarding time – Chronos time vs. Kairos time. Chronos time was used to describe the hands on the clock ticking, the quantitative, concrete measurement of time. This is the experience of *staying* on time, *keeping* time, and constantly trying to beat the clock. Whereas Kairos time was used to describe an experience of timelessness, the qualitative moments that transcend time, when there is actually no comprehension of time at all, when an hour can feel like a minute and vice versa. Kairos is the experience of being able to bend time, to expand, and contract time at will.

Kairos time is not only the preferred experience regarding time, where time is not spent, but rather savored, but it is also the time that gives back. It is how you actually create the experience of *more* time. The question then becomes, how do you move from Chronos time to Kairos time?

You must start by asking yourself what kind of experience your energy around time is creating. What are your thoughts, beliefs, and actions regarding time? To answer this question, let's take a look at your priorities.

Everyone has the same 24 hours in a day, so why is it that some people have the time to get their nails done every week, go to the gym every day, or cook homemade meals for their families, while others do not? Why is it that some people have the time to go to their children's school or sports events, have date nights, or take multiple vacations a year, while others do not? Why is it that some people are willing to work overtime or work nightshift to make a little extra money while others are not? Why is it that some people pay to have their house cleaned or their grass cut while others do it themselves? Why is it that some people make their dreams come true while others do not?

Priorities.

You *are* the creator of your reality. If you never have enough time to pursue your desires, dreams, passions, and purpose, it is simply because you have not prioritized these things. Ask yourself, what are you prioritizing instead?

If it is someone else's desires, or desires based on other people's perceptions of you, then I'm here to tell you that you have it all wrong. Flip your priorities upside down, back in the order that they belong – with your own at the top of your list. You have time for whatever you prioritize. The problem is that most people prioritize a meaningless job, money, social engagements, or even a clean house over their own dreams. Only a select few prioritize their dreams, and that's why only a select few *realize* their dreams.

It's time to decide. What will you prioritize? Make a list of what is important to you and decide now that you will take back your freedom and begin scheduling these priorities first, rather than prioritizing the schedule already laid out for you – the *life* already laid out for you. Because your life is the result of what you prioritize every single day. It is made up of your daily habits.

As James Clear said in his book, Atomic Habits, "The habits you repeat (or don't repeat) every day largely determine your health, wealth, and happiness. Knowing how to change your habits means knowing how to confidently own and manage your days, focus on the behaviors that have the highest impact, and reverse-engineer the life you want." This is how you create the future you want for yourself – in the consistent, daily habits that align with that future version of you. This is how you create your destiny.

You must make the decision to begin prioritizing what you love. And when you do, everything else will fall into place seamlessly. Just as I found more time in my days when I started with writing, the thing I loved most, do what you love most first, too. The true lesson hidden beneath the veil of time that I want to share with you is that time is never wasted doing what you love. To the contrary, this is actually what creates the *perception* of more time. More specifically, it generates energy.

As we've already discussed, everything in the Universe is made up of energy, including you. We know based on the Law of Conservation that energy can neither be created nor destroyed. However, it can certainly change states – it can be transmuted, transformed, or transferred from one object to another. What you put energy into can either absorb that energy or amplify and transfer it back to you.

Prioritizing trivial tasks based on the expectations, needs, and desires of others will deplete your energy and exhaust you. By the time you get around to doing the things you truly want to do for yourself with your NET time, you will find that you no longer have the energy for it.

You do not run out of time, for time is infinite. What you run out of is energy. You have transferred your energy to other people based on *their* needs and desires, or approval. And when you run out of energy, what you then do with your time is irrelevant. You watch television, you scroll social media, you play video games, you order take-out, you nap, etc. This is done to *pass* the time until you are able to rest and re-set, to rejuvenate your energy, which typically involves going to sleep to wake up to a new day.

If you had more energy, what you would choose to do with your time would be very different. But because we have created a world in which the norm is going to work for other people for the first eight hours of our day when we have the most energy, often doing things we don't like doing that takes our energy, and then coming home exhausted, these daily habits of watching and scrolling are what gain momentum and become our habitual behaviors. Neural pathways are strengthened with these repetitive actions and soon these are the things we are doing on autopilot, and this is what creates our life. If this is what you do day after day, you will never regain power over your time.

Taking yourself off of autopilot and making a conscious choice to do something different is how you break free from this pattern. It will involve intentional, conscious choice for a while until the new neural pathways override the old and you have created a new habit. And while you can certainly make the choice to do this in the evenings when you have very little energy left, it will be much more difficult. If you want to make a much quicker, more massive change, you must take a look at who and what you are giving the most productive part of your day. What are you doing on a daily basis when you have the most energy, and who are you doing it for?

Kyle could have kept his job at the commodities dealer and built his business in the evenings and on the weekends, slowly, but surely. He could have woken up every day and continued to give the most productive part of his day, the most energy he had, to his job. He would have then been coming home each night after a long day's work, his energy low, dreading the energy still required of him to build his business. This would have been incredibly short-sighted.

Instead, he took the short-term loss for the long-term gain. He went all in and made building his business his priority. He woke up and did the things he wanted to do first, the things he was excited to do when his energy was high. And because of that, his business was built in a fraction of the time it would have taken if he'd have kept it on the backburner, if he'd prioritized his weekly paycheck over it. We may not have had the means for Kyle to quit his job and go all in, but because he was so sure of his eventual success, we found a way to make it work. And then, the means showed up.

If you were to take back autonomy over your time, and thus your freedom, by scheduling your priorities first, rather than prioritizing the schedule already laid out for you, you would find an infinite amount of time and energy for the things you want to do. Consequently, as you put more focus on the things you want to do, and do them while your energy is high, you will also find that the things that you *need* to do will absorb *less* of your time and energy. These things that you don't necessarily *want* to do will begin to shrink. And just as you saw in the case of my job, as you focus on them less and less, they will sometimes even disappear altogether.

Akin to the instructions you receive before take-off on an airplane, put your own oxygen mask on first, before you try to help anyone else. By focusing on and prioritizing your own needs first, rather than the needs of others, your energy tank gets filled up. You are then able to ride that wave of joy, that overflow of energy, throughout the rest of your day as you easily mark off those other items on your to-do list.

As if on a high, you will begin finding joy even in the most mundane tasks, and like magic, these tasks will seem to get done in a fraction of the time expected, with a sense of ease. Time will seem to float in and all around you, as if you were conducting the orchestra. Herein lies true magic. This is the space where delicious meals get enjoyed, masterpieces get created, million-dollar ideas get invented, and passion projects seemingly become overnight successes.

This is true freedom. It's what we all desire deep down – the freedom to lift all constraints and limitations placed upon your time, and to do *what* you want to do *when* you want to do it. Change your priorities and you will change your life. Focus on your own desires first and you will get your time and energy back. Let go of the illusion of NET time. There is plenty of time to do everything you want to do, and when you do, not only will your energy increase, but everything will become easier, and everything will begin to flow. Yes, even the money.

Money is Energy

I, perhaps like you, spent most of my adult life believing I was not worthy of having a lot of money. I never wanted to be a doctor or a lawyer or an inventor, I didn't have any special physical or creative talents that I believed set me apart, and based on my personality type, I had no business entertaining the idea of a sales career. So, what did I have to offer the world that was worthy of massive compensation?

I always dreamed of being a writer, but writers didn't make a lot of money. So not only did I not pursue my passion of writing, because I believed it wouldn't make money, but instead pursued other career paths that I didn't like, that *also* didn't make a lot of money, because I believed I wasn't worthy of money. It's insanely tragic how dumb we can be.

I landed on racking up over $45,000 worth of student loan debt to get a master's degree in Human Resources Leadership shortly after finishing undergrad. I signed away my life before the prefrontal cortex in my brain, which is responsible for critical thinking, was even fully developed. I chose HR because it seemed like the easiest route to make a decent living – not a *great* living, because whatever skills and talents I had didn't deserve that, but a *decent* one. I rationalized that HR was a smart choice because if I worked hard enough, one day, far down the road, I might be able to make six figures. And honestly, that was all I could ever dream of, because I came from a family that made less than six figures. So, to me, that was the epitome of success. Money, to me, six figures to be exact, meant freedom.

However, once I had that amount of student loan debt and a degree that I was now obligated to use, I had no freedom at all. I was indebted to a lender, tied to those monthly payments for, what would appear to have been, the entirety of my adult life. The high monthly payments took a good portion of that *decent* paycheck, making the whole idea of freedom null and void.

Here's where I went wrong: *It was all about the money.* Every single decision I made was about the money. None of my choices had anything to do with what I *wanted* to do, what I actually *desired* for my life. Instead, my decisions revolved around figuring out what I *could* do that would be the *least painful* for the most amount of money.

How different my life could have been if I would have had enough sense to just stop for a moment and ask myself, what is it that I think that $100k a year down the line is going to do for me? Maybe then it would have led to me questioning what I *actually* wanted out of life. Because what I *thought* the money was going to bring me was a sense of freedom, but if you are being forced to do something you do not want to do for eight to nine hours a day for 49 to 50 weeks a year, for at least 40 or so years, it is the *opposite* of freedom.

What I learned that changed my entire life, and what I would like to share with you, perhaps before you get too far in over your head trying to do the "smart" thing, is that it is *never actually about the money*. This is where so many people go wrong. You must actually remove the money from the equation entirely if you want to stand a chance at living a life of freedom.

Don't take my word for it. Take a look at the most uber-successful people in the world. Study them. Read their stories. Most of them have a common thread in their experience, which is that they didn't start doing it for the money. They started for the *love* of their craft and their advice is always to find something that you *love* and eventually, the money will follow.

This is how you obtain *real* freedom. This is how you obtain *real* success. When you find something that you love, something that you are inherently interested in, something that you are obsessed with, that you could do all the time, just for the fun of it – that is where genius lies.

Niche down in whatever it is that lights you up and an extraordinary life will follow, along with extraordinary success and extraordinary money. And by extraordinary money, I'm not talking about $100k, I'm talking about *limitless abundance*.

You've likely heard the bible verse, "For the love of money is the root of all evil." - 1 Timothy 6:10. This is another thing I believe the bible got right. Please do not get this twisted – Money, *itself*, is not the root of all evil. Money is a neutral resource. Like everything, it contains aspects of polarity and duality. It can be used for all kinds of purposes, just as a knife can be used to cut open a package, cut open a body for surgery, or cut someone's throat. But the *love* of money – *this* will ruin your life. It will have you doing things you don't want to do, with and for people you don't like, to buy things you don't even really want, to impress – *who*, exactly? And you won't even realize until it's all over how little, if any of it, even mattered.

Money is not real. It is only paper, after all. It holds no intrinsic value. If you held on to a $100 bill from someone's life savings in 1930 until today, you would see this firsthand. If it hadn't disintegrated already, that same $100 bill wouldn't last a week in today's time. Hold onto it for another one hundred years and you would likely find that the paper holds *no* value, whatsoever, as digital currency will likely be the only means of exchange.

To help you conceptualize how truly worthless money is, let's take it all the way back to its roots. Before money was invented as a medium for exchange, people used to barter with cattle, grains, salt, and even seashells! Can you imagine it, seashells! Eventually it was precious metals, with gold becoming the most coveted.

The dollar bill was invented as a lightweight, portable option to represent the gold someone owned. Known as the Gold Standard, governments only printed as much money as they had in gold so that at any time, that dollar bill could be exchanged for what was really believed to be valuable – which of course, was the gold it represented.

However, during the Great Depression in the 1920's, countries abandoned the gold standard altogether and began printing more and more money out of thin air, far more money than there was gold to back it up. This has continued to occur today, with the government consistently printing more money "as needed" to address economic issues. This is why the dollar bill is not stable and holds no real value, because it doesn't *actually* represent anything. Thus, we have inflation and recession.

Money is not real. The only reason we trust in its buying power is because we have all collectively agreed upon it. It is only our acceptance of it, and collective belief in it, that keeps the entire system from collapsing upon itself.

Today, digital currency has taken over and there certainly is not enough paper currency or precious metals in the world to back all of the digits everyone sees when they open their computer screens to check their savings and investment balances. Again, *it is not real*. It is just numbers on a screen that can be wiped out at any time. And if your truest desire is to see numbers on a screen, I can guarantee that you will live a sad, sad life.

The real question that you need to ask yourself is not how much money you want, but what you think that money will do for you. Why do you want the money? You may land on ideas such as freedom, health, and happiness. To which I would reply, money is the byproduct of that life, not the other way around. As a matter of fact, if you chase money for money's sake, it will often be at the *expense* of your freedom, health, and happiness. You think money will allow you to do the things you love, but what if you *just* decided to do the things you loved now, without the money? Could you do it?

Even if the things you love require money to do, the fact that you have a love for something, an interest in it, means other people do too. It means other people pay money to do it too. Surely you can see the opportunity there.

You are meant to have everything your heart desires, but you cannot work toward your desires if you prioritize money over them. By hoisting money up on a pedestal and putting it in between you and what you ultimately want out of life, you give away your power to an outside entity. And as we've already discussed, what you desire is not outside of you, but within you.

No matter how many people try to convince you otherwise, you *can* have everything you want, and that includes making money doing what you love, as long as it doesn't *start* with the money in mind, but instead, starts with what you *love* in mind. This is *how* you build a life of freedom, health, and happiness. You find something that lights you up. You learn everything there is to learn about it. You practice working with or on it. You become an expert at or on it. And then, you find a way to niche down, and monetize the knowledge you have gained.

There are professional video game players that make a million dollars a year. There are influencers and bloggers that talk about clothes and make-up that are multi-millionaires. There are interior decorators, clothes designers, stylists, fitness instructors, chefs, and nutritionists that make millions. To say that you cannot make money doing something you love is incredibly short-sighted. It is simply a lie.

The difference between those people – the video game players, the influencer and bloggers, the fitness instructors, and *you*, is that they found something they loved, something that they would do every day for the pure enjoyment of it, for no money at all. Then they began doing it every day, *not* for the money, but because it brought them joy to do so. Money, then, became the byproduct of their expertise, fueled by passion.

Money, like everything else in this world, is just energy, and is largely determined by the energetic frequency you hold around the idea of it. You can see this so clearly in regards to people that find themselves on the receiving end of money after being poor for most of their lives.

Over 60% of lottery winners have lost all of their money within two years of getting it. The winners likely spent an entire lifetime believing they weren't worthy of money, so when they got it, they couldn't hold on to the energetic frequency of money. They were not in alignment with it. Their actions in losing the money was simply a reflection of their belief system within. You also see this with many professional athletes, particularly those that come from low-income homes. They earn millions and then somehow quickly squander it all away and end up filing for bankruptcy.

In the book, *The Big Leap*, Gayle Hendricks describes it as an upper limit problem that we all face when we get something we think we want that we have always thought was out of our reach. In the book, he states, "The upper limit problem is our universal human tendency to sabotage ourselves when we have exceeded the artificial upper limit we have placed on ourselves." We may think that we want something, but we don't actually believe it's possible for us, so we can't hold onto it when we get it.

When one believes that they will never have more than a certain amount in their bank account, they never do. If it happens that they obtain more than they believe they can have, all of a sudden, an unexpected emergency comes up.

When one believes money is difficult to make, it is difficult for them to make. When one believes money is difficult to hold onto, it is difficult for them to hold onto. When one believes that no matter how hard they work that they can't ever get ahead, they never get ahead. When one believes they are not talented enough, resourced enough, or determined enough, or that they don't have anything to offer to make money, they are never talented enough, resourced enough, determined enough, or have anything to offer that makes money.

The same is true in regards to the opposite. When one truly believes they are talented enough to charge over the market rate for their services, people get in line to pay them that rate. When one truly believes that their work is worthy of a higher salary, their request will be granted and they will receive the amount of money they desire to be paid. When one truly believes that their work is exceptional, they make exceptional money. When one truly believes they can make money in their sleep, they wake up to more money in their bank account.

Your beliefs are self-fulfilling prophecies. They affect the way you show up in the world. And how you show up – your actions, backed by your beliefs, determines your reality. If you can align your energy with your desires, by thinking about what it is that you desire, believing you are worthy of it, and continually taking action steps toward it, you will become a powerful, unstoppable force. Energy will move at your will. You will eventually see more digits on your screen, along with *all kinds* of other resources, to support your vision.

The Universe, which is *all* energy, is only, and always, responding to *your* energy. Your energy is quite literally affecting the energy of *everything* around you. This includes money, which will always match your energy.

Say it with me: *Money flows to me freely and abundantly*. Believe it. Learn it. Live it. Take the action steps to create the life you desire, and watch the money flow in support of your vision. Because the life you desire is not selfish, it is your path to abundance. And abundance is your contribution to the world.

An Abundant Universe

"Look deep into nature and you will understand everything better." - Albert Einstein.

The Universe is abundant by nature. It is constantly expanding, shapeshifting, and evolving before our very eyes, to create all that we see, touch, taste, smell, and hear all around us. Information, communication, literacy, connectivity, intelligence, technology, energy, food supply, water supply, human life, and human life span – it is all growing and expanding.

In studying our planet, it is easy to see that the way nature is abundant is through diversity. Entire ecosystems thrive – coral reefs, forests, prairies, you name it – they are built on interdependent relationships which create the conditions that keep the whole system healthy.

A variety of plants and animals means there are a variety of different resources to nourish, to heal, to grow, and to flourish. And since each organism creates an abundance of the particular resources that they create, that overflow can then be shared. It is a system of abundance and generosity, rather than one of lack and scarcity.

Organisms within these ecosystems learn quickly that if they work together, they can get what they need and they, themselves, serve a great purpose in creating what other organisms need as well. It is a system formulated on personal abundance – the ability to give easily based on overflow, once one's own needs are sufficiently met. Each organism holds a uniquely intrinsic value based on its diversity and ability to create that personal abundance in its area of genius.

You are one with the Universe, one with nature. As an extension of nature, a fragmented piece of the Universe, you are designed to be abundant, too.

If you aren't, the only reason is because you do not believe that you are. Perhaps you do not believe it is necessary to be abundant or that it is not right to want abundance for yourself. Perhaps you do not believe it is possible, or that you are worthy. At the root of it, you do not believe that your diversity makes you special. You may even feel that your diversity is what makes you less than. But what I am here to remind you is that you are incredibly special just because you are *you* and no one else is exactly like you.

Someone once said, "Everybody is a genius. But if you judge a fish by its ability to climb a tree, it will live its whole life believing that it is stupid."

We have created a society that is hell-bent on conformity, on hiding that which makes us different from one another. We have shunned our unique gifts and inner desires in an attempt to follow the well-paved paths set before us that everyone else is following. It was the great Stoic philosopher Seneca who said, "We should not, like sheep, follow the herd of creatures in front of us, making our way where others go, not where we ought to go." This was said 20 centuries ago – *2,000 years ago*. And yet the majority of us still blindly follow the herd, all the while believing that we are not abundant because we are stupid, because we do not excel within one of the perfect little categories set before us.

While we may admire those select, special few that step off the well-beaten path to go after their dreams and make something different of themselves, those who show us a different way to live, who show up as their natural and authentic self in pursuit of their dreams, we are often too scared to do so ourselves. We are too embarrassed to even try. We feel it to be pretentious to even consider that we *could possibly* be that special. So rather than embracing that which makes us different, the majority of us compete for the same ideal life, even though it is anything but ideal, and not at all what we really want.

The lack of diversity among us means that we are all competing for the same resources. Competition and rivalry create separateness and scarcity. Fear takes over, survival instincts set in, and resources are hoarded, rather than shared. Soon the organisms in this environment – people, in this case – do not have what they need to survive, much less thrive.

We could learn a thing or two by looking to nature for guidance. There is simply no need for competition when we are all so very different in the desires, talents, and gifts we have to share with the world. Remember, no two humans are exactly the same – this is by divine design. We are meant to niche down until we find the exact thing that lights us up, that makes us excited to learn and to share, that makes us magnetic to the people and resources we require to thrive, and creates overflow in our lives and in the world.

No matter what anyone tells you, no market is too saturated and not everything has been done before. The simple fact is, it has not been done by *you*. And no one else can do it *quite like you*. You must disregard the lie that others are too much further ahead, that you are too far behind. As motivational speaker Les Brown said, "You are never too old to set a new goal or to dream a new dream."

Regardless of where you are starting out, you are steps ahead of someone else who has not yet begun, and they can benefit from the knowledge you've gained. No matter where you are in your journey, you are ready to share what you've learned with the world. When you show up honestly as your fully expressed, authentic self in the area of your genius, there is no limit to the abundance you can create.

But you can't do that if you resolve to live within the world of conformity that we have collectively created. Not everyone thrives in an occupation already created. Not everyone thrives being micromanaged or working in groups or even working away from home. Not everyone thrives waking up to an alarm clock at 6am to go to a job five days a week for eight hours a day. Not everyone thrives following the rules that society has established.

If you want to show up as your fully expressed, authentic self, the first thing you must do is ditch the "rule book" that tells you how you are supposed to behave, and find your *own* way, which will most likely be *off* the beaten path. If you want to create your own personal abundance, you must re-write the rules for your own life.

Rules are Merely Suggestions

After my sister passed, the television station where she worked held a memorial in her honor. It was a beautiful tribute to Dana that allowed my family to see her through the eyes of others. While we knew Dana was a force to be reckoned with, it was eye-opening to see the influence she'd had on those that she worked with as well, to see how much they all admired and adored her.

Dana was easy to love. She had so much personality that set her apart, and her authenticity shined through in everything she said and did. She was the type that told you how it was, always, even the hard truths. And while it wasn't always well-received in the moment, for most, it made them love her even more. Dana chose to always and only speak her truth, which often hit right at the core of the matter, and for that reason her word was like gospel to anyone that sought out her advice.

A common theme among the stories told about Dana was her hilarious inability, or perhaps more accurately, unwillingness, to follow some of the most basic rules at work. We knew from teenage Dana that she didn't care much for rules and this apparently carried over into adulthood as well.

Around the office, Dana had taken on the nickname "West Coast" due to the fact that she never made it to work on time. So much so, that in the ten plus years she'd worked there, she had never carried a key to the building. She simply would never be the first one to arrive or the last one to leave. So, what did she need with a key?

Dana's boss described how he pulled up to the building one morning to see an anomaly. Dana, at work before anyone else. For the first time ever, she'd gotten up early to take her stepson, Cameron, to school because Shawn had an early morning meeting he couldn't miss. So, there was Dana, keyless, sitting outside on the grass by the front door, typing away on her laptop.

Her boss said she looked up at him with a big smile on her face, unphased by the circumstances. After he'd let her in the building, he told her if she couldn't find her key, he would be happy to get her another one so that this didn't happen to her again. To which Dana promptly replied, "Nah, this will never happen again."

Dana never really had a good excuse for being late, she simply couldn't get out of bed that morning, or had to stop for breakfast. She wouldn't stay extra late to "make up the time" either. She would barely offer an apology, but if prompted, would promise to try to get there earlier. When her husband, Shawn, would ask her what her plan was to follow through on this, she would shrug her shoulders and say, "Oh, I'm not really going to. What are they gonna do, fire me?"

Her behavior had become a running joke and a source for bets around the office about how late she may be on any particular given day. They'd often tell her meetings started earlier than they actually did just to ensure that she would be there on time.

Dana was a high-earning employee, who produced more than the average, and always got her work done. Perhaps her boss wouldn't have turned a blind eye if that weren't the case. But if you ask me? It was Dana's flat-out assuredness over the fact that nobody was going to tell her what to do, that made it so. There was no doubt in her mind. There was no stutter in her apology. There was no break in her tardiness.

Dana's thoughts, beliefs, and actions all aligned on this one fact – she could be late if she damn well pleased. And therefore, she was a force to be reckoned with.

Rules are really just suggestions. This was one of Dana's favorite sayings. And anyone that knew her would tell you that she truly believed it. It's how she lived her entire life. Sold out? No problem, she'd sneak in. Bad seats? No worries, she'd sit closer until someone made her move. No swimming after dark? Catch me if you can! Invitation only? The name's Smith, *but* it could also be under Brown. No parking? She'd find a window seat to watch for the tow truck. No time off? Can't help it if you're sick.

Dana believed she could get away with anything, and that it would be easy for her to do so. It never seemed to affect her when she was ever-so occasionally called out for her behavior because she was completely unbothered by other people's expectations or opinions of her. She didn't mind apologizing, *if* necessary, but she *never* asked for permission.

Instead, she took consistent action, based on her belief that she could always do what she damn well pleased, and it strengthened her belief in the idea. Every time she took action that aligned with that belief, it became more and more a part of who she was, and reality reflected her internal belief back to her. She had to do less and less apologizing as other people began believing right along with her, and accepting the reality she had created - she really could damn well do what she pleased. The proof was in her many years of doing just that.

If one has a belief about how things should be, but doesn't take the corresponding actions to align with that belief to solidify it in the real world, perhaps due to already created spoken or unspoken rules, whether real or perceived, then their belief simply is not strong enough to alter reality.

Action, backed by belief, is how you build up the proof for yourself and others to make it real. *This* is how you alter reality – not just in aligning your thoughts and your beliefs, but in taking the corresponding action to solidify it in the 3D, material world in which we live. This is how the rules of the world are created, by someone bold enough to take action based on their thoughts and beliefs about how things should be. Be bold. Otherwise, the rules you and your children, and your grandchildren will be required to follow will be written without your input or consent.

They say when someone you love dies, the best way you can honor them is to take on the traits you loved most about them. When I decided I was free to spend the first few hours of my work day writing rather than working, and not giving a damn what anyone had to say about it, I was no doubt channeling Dana. This is something I do all the time now that she is gone. I so often find myself thinking, *what would Dana do?*

I'm sad to say I didn't do this when Dana was alive. In fact, I prided myself on being the exact opposite of her in every way. I was easy going and agreeable. I went with the flow and put other people's needs and desires above my own every single time. The fact that we always had to go where Dana wanted to go, do what Dana wanted to do, eat where Dana wanted to eat, drove me mad, *absolutely bonkers*. I often thought she was selfish and self-centered based on the way she acted. We got in many fights about this over the years because we were *so* different, because she was always pushing me to do the things I didn't want to do, or didn't think I could, or *should* do, and insisting on the things she wanted over anyone else's desires. What she wanted was of the upmost importance and she didn't care to make it known.

But guess what? Dana was right. After she was gone, I got to see her, truly see her in all of her glory in a way that I couldn't when she was still here. I could see the full timeline of her life and see how beautiful it was that she did everything she wanted to do. She lived more in her 38 years than most people lived in sixty, seventy, eighty, even ninety years. It was as if she knew subconsciously that she only had a short time here. Which, of course, is true of all of us.

The fact that I'd wasted so much time being annoyed and frustrated with Dana actually had nothing to do with her, and everything to do with *myself*. She triggered me, because somewhere deep down inside, I wanted to be her. I wanted to have the confidence and the audacity to assert my desires and to shamelessly get whatever it was that I wanted too – to be so sure of what I wanted that I demanded respect, demanded that the energy move in the direction I willed it.

But the truth is that I was just too scared – too scared of what people might think, of being judged, too scared that I might fail, that I wasn't good enough, or that I wasn't important enough, or deserving enough. I was too scared to be the main character in my own life.

But now, Dana serves as my reminder, and I hope she can serve as yours too. Life is short. Live free. Stop asking for permission. Stop worrying about what anyone else thinks. It's YOUR life. Put yourself first and prioritize *your* desires, because freedom is not something you are granted externally, it is an inside job. Freedom is a state of mind, anchored into reality by action.

The Power of How

"But I can't, because…" I'm sure this thought has gone through your mind more than once while reading this book, especially during this section. I can almost read your thoughts now, "But I have a job, I have responsibilities, I have bills. I can't just throw it all away to pursue my dreams. Following my dreams may pay off in the long run, but make-believe won't pay my rent next week."

And you are right, it won't. I'm not asking you to throw it all away and move to Hollywood or quit your job and start a business. Those are bold moves, and I certainly was not that bold either. Who I was and who I wanted to be had *miles* between them and I had to build up my belief slowly over time through consistent, everyday action. You may need to do this too based on your risk tolerance. If you're like my husband, a big risk all at once was motivating, perhaps even necessary. But if you are like me, a big risk all at once could have the opposite effect. History may favor the bold, but bridging the gap between who you are and who you want to be may require small leaps over time for some, rather than one great, big massive leap all at once.

Luckily, small changes yield big results. Remember the butterfly effect? One small change can alter *everything*. Let's start with that one small change.

When you find yourself thinking, "I can't do what I want to do because of X," replace it with the question, "How can I find a way to do what I want to do *now*, along with X?" Replacing, "I can't," with "How can I," changes what you are seeking, and you always want to be seeking solutions, rather than problems.

Remember that whether you think you can, or you think you can't, you are right. Thinking of all of your limitations and constraints will never help you realize your dreams. What you ask your brain to look for, it will seek proof of. So, never say, "I can't" in regards to something you desire. Always ask, "How can I…"

"How can I fit this into my schedule? How can I make this easier? How can I make this less scary? How can I enjoy this?" Whatever the obstacle, instead of focusing on the obstacle, ask *how* you can get around it. Even if the answer does not immediately come to you, eventually, the answer *will* arrive. This is the power of *How*.

Quitting my job to become an author before we had the means to do so would have been a disaster for me. But I didn't need to quit my job to start being a writer. I just had to stop telling myself that I couldn't write because I had a job, and start asking myself instead, how can I be a writer now, *along with* having a job? This tiny shift in my thinking changed *everything*.

I only ask that you make tiny shifts as well to get started. Small, sustainable changes create massive shifts in your reality. What starts as just a few minutes each day grows over time. On the other hand, if you try to completely overhaul your entire life in one night, you stand the chance of getting burnt out before you even begin. You may have too much resistance to it and may not be able to get your belief behind it. Like me, you may need to build up evidence to believe in its probability and to get your actions into alignment with it.

Let's say that you have decided a priority for yourself is to get fit. Perhaps the future you, that you envision, wakes up at 5am and works out every morning. But the current you not only hates working out, but also hates mornings. If you try to start this intense habit overnight, you will likely fail. You may do it once. You may even do it twice. But you will not do it long term. You will probably get overwhelmed and frustrated and quit before you even really get started.

Instead, ask yourself, "How can I find a way to enjoy getting fit? How can I make getting fit easier?" The best way to get things rolling in the direction of your dreams is to decide on what you can do now that is small and easy, as well as enjoyable. Commit to just a few minutes each day to focus on your desire and take one small step forward. Make small goals and celebrate every time you follow through on your plans. Build up the proof that you can follow through on your promises and build up your belief in yourself each time you follow through on the smallest actions.

Maybe it's going for a ten minute walk every morning. You may find some days that you want to walk longer, you may eventually work up to a thirty minute walk every day, or even miraculously find yourself running one day. This is how it works, not in trying to run a marathon on day one, even if that is your ultimate goal, but by taking small, measured steps toward your goal and doing so with consistency.

Getting fit could also look like lifting weights for only five minutes a day.

As you feel your muscles tightening and becoming defined, and as you've carved out the space and time for weightlifting, maybe you end up doing more than five minutes a day. Find something small, something that you can not only find the time for, but the energy for, and stick with it. Then, watch as it grows naturally. Take your focus away from quick results and instead focus on the long term, that which is sustainable, and it will eventually lead to accomplishing what you desire.

When you envision the future you, perhaps she eats fresh, organic fruits and vegetables every day. She meal preps and takes a healthy lunch to work each day. She plans and cooks healthy dinners for her family.

The current you, however, hates grocery shopping, isn't great at cooking, grabs fast food for lunch every day, and orders take-out for dinner regularly. That's a large gap to bridge. So, start small.

What's one thing you can change in your schedule now to get momentum moving in the direction of your desire? Maybe it could be making one homemade meal a week. Schedule that one meal a week into your weekly routine. When are you going to plan the meal? When are you going to go to the grocery store? When are you going to cook it? Plan ahead, and then stick to your plan. Make it a priority to stick to this one small change and leave it at that, *for now*.

Eventually, you will get used to making this one weekly homemade meal and it will become quicker and easier. It will become habitual. Like clockwork, you will know exactly when you will plan it each week, how long it will take you to shop, and to cook, and to clean up afterward. You will have made the space for this habit to grow and overtime, you will begin to develop staple meals. You will know what pantry ingredients to keep on hand, and what fresh ingredients are needed each week. Eventually, you will hardly have to think about it at all. It will just become a part of your routine and a part of your life. It will become a part of you. And this is when the magic happens.

Once that one meal becomes a habitual behavior, something that becomes a part of you, and you *become* a person who cooks for her family, you will likely want to add on a second meal per week, and so on. As it becomes easier to make these meals, you may find yourself *wanting* to double your ingredients and start having leftovers to take for lunches, or meals to freeze for later. You may find that you begin to enjoy getting up on Saturday mornings and going to farmer's markets for fresh fruits and vegetables, and even enjoying the taste of them more. You may find that meal prepping is not as hard or time consuming as you once thought it to be.

That few minutes a day to start, if done consistently, will take you further than you could have ever imagined. What you focus on expands and whether it's cooking, or working out, or writing a book, or building a business, the amount of time you dedicate to it will increase over time once you've carved out the space for it. Slow and steady wins the race every time.

What's important is that you don't quit on this one small change. You will falter. You will fail. You will fall off the bandwagon on an exceptionally stressful week. If you are trying to lose weight and are weighing yourself regularly, you will find many days that the number on the scale jumps up.

Success is never linear. It is found in the recovery, in the willingness to start again, in how quickly you learn from your mistakes and bounce back, rather than allowing them to snowball. Remember Kanter's Law – everything looks like a failure in the middle. Those that don't accept failure, but instead quickly get back on track, will find success sooner. So, find that one, small thing again, and make the decision to begin again.

In the book, *Outliers*, Malcom Gladwell popularized the idea of "The Rule of 100" which is based on research that concludes 100 hours of dedicated focus or practice is what is required to obtain mastery on a subject. He points out that 100 hours is roughly 18 minutes a day for a year, and concludes that it only takes 18 minutes, if done consecutively each and every day, to master a subject or a skill. *Everyone* has 18 minutes a day.

Extraordinary people understand that it is not what you do with great time and effort every once in a while, but the small things you do habitually, each and every day, that defines who you are and determines your success. These small things add up over time. Focus on what you can do every single day with as little resistance as possible to move you toward your goals.

Your actions will build momentum, and once all aligns, once you are fully embodying the you that you desire to be, something magical occurs. Just as $25k was handed to us unexpectedly when I made the decision to buy a home, began believing I actually *could* do it, and took action steps toward it, you, too, will receive assistance that far outweighs any amount of planning or effort that you could put in as well.

That's because the *actual* "how" is never really up to you. Your job is only to get into alignment with the thing that you desire. You do this through your thoughts, your beliefs, and yes, your actions. But how your manifestation comes to fruition will always be through ways in which you could have never imagined. Because it's not just up to you. You are a part of something bigger. Something that shows you what you need to do next and provides you with an infinite number of resources to do it. Some people call this grace, some may call it divine intervention, some may even call it a miracle.

I call it *flow*.

FLOW

How your feelings create reality.

PART IV

Flow

\<verb\>

To proceed or be produced smoothly, continuously, and effortlessly.

NEW OXFORD AMERICAN DICTIONARY

PART 4: FLOW

"We suffer more in our imagination than in reality."

SENECA

It was May of 2023. I sat at a picnic table in the mid-morning sun beneath a blooming maple tree with my laptop in front of me. Writing *this* chapter of my book, actually.

It was a year after my daughter, Khloe, was born and nine months after I had quit my job. My son, Knox, then four, was attending forest school a few days a week at a nature preserve. Since he only went for half a day, and it was a thirty-minute drive from our home, on the days that he attended school, I would take my laptop and write while I waited for him to be released.

These were my favorite days of the week. Since I had nothing but nature all around me and no kids or internet to distract me, it was easy to get into and stay in the flow of writing. However, on this particular day, as I was trying to write the final chapter of my book *on* flow, *nothing* was flowing. The irony, while not lost on me, hardly had me laughing.

Nine months ago, I had asked my husband to take a leap of faith with me. To believe in me, the same way in which I'd always believed in him. To support me in going after my dreams, as I'd always supported him in going after his. Now that his business was such a success, he was making more than enough money to support us while I took the time and space to go after my dream of becoming a best-selling author – A *New York Times Best Selling Author*, to be precise.

Of course, I realized that my dream was crazy. Not many people made it big as a writer, certainly not *New York Times Best Seller* big. But I had to remind him, *and* myself, that not many people made it big as an entrepreneur either. If I could believe in his crazy dreams, he could believe in mine. And in asking him to do so, I had asked myself to dig deep and to do the same – for quite possibly the first time ever, to really and truly believe in myself, and to go all in on my dreams.

How could I not go all in? My husband had his first million-dollar year in business and we'd had our second baby. It was such a seamless transition for me to simply not go back to work after my maternity leave was up. It all made so much sense, everything falling perfectly into place. Not only would I have the two hours a day required to take my son to and from the school we'd chosen for him in another town, but I'd also be able to take more off Kyle's plate to help the business grow and thrive. And most importantly, I'd be able to use the flexibility of my new schedule to finish writing my first book and begin my career as an author.

The stars had aligned in such a magnificent way to allow for it all to happen. It felt like it was meant to be, as if the whole Universe had conspired in my favor to bring me to this point in time.

But while it had felt as though destiny were unfolding, it had not, in fact, brought me to the realization of my dreams. Instead, it had brought me to this moment, stuck staring at my laptop, experiencing a prolonged bout of writer's block. To a place where all the magic around me was slowly dissipating, as if the spell had been lifted, and reality was settling back in. The real world was calling for my return and it was going to ring, and ring, and ring until I woke up from my fairytale dream and answered the call back to reality.

Here's what happened…

We closed out 2022 on the biggest *money* high of our lives. Our goal for the year had been to make a million dollars profit, and we'd made well-over that goal. It was a miracle.

In hindsight, it was actually inflation, caused by the government's response to the Covid-19 pandemic. Supply had gone down and demand had gone up, up, and up. Demand had gone through the roof, and companies were paying just about anything to get their product on shelves.

At the beginning of 2023, however, the pendulum swung back in the opposite direction – the recession hit, and the freight business was the first to feel the effects. Stock wasn't selling out, and companies were shipping smaller amounts of product. They were requiring less than truck loads, some were parceling it out themselves, and many were able to handle the smaller volume in-house, as opposed to having to outsource to a third-party.

We had always claimed that logistics was a recession-proof business. Product was always going to have to move, period. And, that was true. But, when you're a third-party outsourcing company, it means you go from handling massive amounts of volume during inflation, to handling whatever scraps you can during recession, and doing so on the cheap just to keep the business. We'd scaled our company to handle the additional volume, so when it suddenly dropped, the situation quickly became dire.

We thought we had done all the right things with the money we'd made in 2022. At the end of that year, we had invested a good amount of money into our retirement accounts and into funds for the kid's futures. We had paid off all of our debt, aside from my student loans, having only held on to them due to the fact that they weren't gaining interest at the time, and the remaining mortgage on our million-dollar home, which we'd paid down to just under $500k (we were patting ourselves on the back for that one seeing as how we'd only been in the home for 2 years). We'd paid off everything else, including the majority of the balance due on the pool and outdoor kitchen we were having built. We knew there were just a few final bills coming when the construction was fully complete, which we thought we'd put enough money aside in preparation for.

However, as the recession hit in quarter one of 2023, we realized we were bringing in only about half of what we were averaging weekly in 2022. We didn't panic. We assumed it was just a few slow weeks and that it would turn around. And besides, half of over a million dollars is nothing to scoff at.

But it didn't turn around. It kept getting worse, and doing so quickly. Our profits dwindled. In the span of just three weeks, we went from barely making enough profit to pay our bills, to the next week not making a profit at all, to the following week in which we couldn't even cover payroll. We started flying through our savings.

And then, we got our tax bill. We had put aside 25% of our profits, assuming that would be enough, or at least close to enough, considering we'd paid quarterly taxes throughout the year, had taxes withheld on the w-2 earnings we'd paid ourselves, and had expenses to report. The truth, which I am ashamed to admit, is that we just didn't really understand the new tax bracket we had landed in. We'd simply never dealt with this kind of money before, and although we had given our accountant the heads up about what we were on track to make and asked for his advice, he didn't advise us to do anything differently than what we'd always done.

Our 2022 tax bill came along with our quarter one tax bill for 2023, since it was due just a short time later and was based, of course, off what we'd made in the prior year – *not* what we were currently making. In total, we owed the government a little over $417k. The bulk of this was due immediately and the rest in just a few short weeks.

We didn't have it. We were short to the tune of over $150k *and* we'd gone through our six-month emergency savings already just to pay our bills and payroll. Based on the current state of affairs, we also didn't know if we were ever going to make any money again. As if on cue, right around this time, the final bills for the construction we'd had on our home started rolling in, as well as Knox's school tuition (which was as expensive as some college tuitions), that we'd already signed a binding contract agreeing to pay.

We didn't have enough to cover any of these expenses. We would have to pull it from our investments and retirement accounts, which meant hefty fees and even more taxes owed, and it would leave us with nothing. One questionable financial decision stacked upon another had fallen in line with a cruel act of nature – the recession – which had created the perfect financial storm for us.

In what felt like the blink of an eye, we were on the brink of losing it all. This beautiful dream world that we'd created for ourselves, our business, our dream home, and everything we'd built, was in jeopardy.

Why hadn't we saved more for a rainy day? Why had we spent so frivolously? Why hadn't we seen this coming? How do you go from making over a million dollars in one year to worrying about losing your home? These questions swirled in my mind, on repeat, making me physically ill.

We were going to have to cut salaries and fire people, and since we'd hired friends and family, that was an even harder pill to swallow, even worse than losing everything ourselves. My nerves were shot. The heavy weight of anxiety sat on my chest. I was exhausted from waking up all hours of the night, in a sweat, the pit of my stomach twisting and churning, as though I'd eaten something rotten.

I knew logically there were worse things than this. Having lost my sister, I'd gone through something much worse just a short time ago. Knox, Khloe, Kyle, and I were all healthy and safe. Logically, I understood this. But while this panicked feeling may have been irrational, it was still all-consuming. I couldn't shake it.

I'll never forget Kyle's face as he looked out our kitchen window, dark circles under his eyes, rubbing his temples. I imagined his head throbbed like mine from a string of sleepless nights and the lack of appetite.

"Look at him," he'd said to me, nodding out the window toward our son, who had a huge smile plastered on his face, knee deep in a pile of dirt left behind from the construction on the pool. "He could care less about any of this," he'd motioned around him to the house. "All he needs to be happy is a pile of dirt."

Kyle was right. If we lost it all, it wouldn't make one bit of a difference to our son. He'd be excited about the new dirt at the next house, no matter how much smaller the yard was. It made me think of all the silly things we'd spent so much money on, all the things we could be just as happy without.

And here I was, the one making all of the financial decisions, the one spending most of the money we'd made, without even a job to help. While I had spent all of these months writing, I could have been doing something that made money. I could have been building something of my own, something to help support us. Instead, here I'd sat, day after day, wasting my time working on this stupid book. On this book that I probably would never even finish.

How could I possibly finish it now? The entire book was about creating the life of your dreams. And now that it looked like we were going to lose everything, I realized I hadn't even done that for myself. Maybe I could retitle it, *How to LOSE the Life of Your Dreams as Quickly as You Created It*. Very Catchy.

Even if I did finish the book, who would read it? No one. I certainly didn't have a following to market it to, and a book deal for a first-time author, especially one without a platform, was a one-in-a-million chance. I had been kidding myself, living in this dream world. I'd wasted so much precious time. *You can't make money writing.* I'd known it all along, and here I was, back at square one, back at that belief all over again. *God, please help me. Help me find a way to turn this all around.*

"Hi there! I'm so sorry about all the commotion. We're setting up for a big event this weekend. I just wanted to come over and apologize. I can see you're trying to concentrate, and here we are making all of this noise!"

Snapping out of my dark thoughts, I was pulled back into reality – back to the picnic table, underneath the maple tree, basking in the mid-morning sun. A woman – blonde, pretty, and bubbly – had popped up in front of me, seemingly out of thin air. *Yes, I was trying to concentrate,* I'd thought hastily to myself.

She held out her hand to shake mine, "Sorry, I'm Tavia – I'm the director here." I reluctantly held out my hand as well as I hurriedly introduced myself. I'd hoped she would get the hint and move on quickly. I hadn't written a lick and time was of the essence now, now that it looked like I'd have to go back to work.

But she continued on, oblivious to my inner dialogue, "What are ya workin' on there?" she asked, as she nodded toward my laptop. "Are you a writer?" *I wish,* I'd thought.

"No, I'm not. I mean, I guess I *fancy* myself a writer, but… I've never actually finished anything I've started," *And I never will,* I completed the sentence in my head. "So, you know, I think that's kind of a prerequisite for calling yourself a writer." I finished, giving a short laugh, trying to sound light hearted, and not like my dreams were in the midst of being torn to shreds.

"Ah, I love to write, too. You know, my friend – her name's Ann Patchett – you may have heard of her?" I shook my head, *no.* It sounded somewhat familiar, but didn't land.

"Well, she's a writer. Ann and I grew up together. She actually donated a signed copy of her newest book that we're going to be auctioning off at the event tomorrow. You may have heard of it – *Tom Lake?*" She looked to me again for recognition. I had none.

I nodded my head, *yes*, this time though, because she seemed so sure that I should know it. I didn't follow any local writers. Of course, I hardly followed any famous writers either, for that matter. *Probably because I'm not really a writer. A real writer would read more. They'd certainly know of all the successful local writers*, I thought, internally punching myself once again.

"Oh wow, that's…awesome." I said stupidly, unable to think of a better adjective. *And I call myself a writer* – the thought sent an uppercut to my jaw.

I didn't want to hear any more about her event. I knew what she was getting at, and I wasn't going to come. Never mind the fact that social events were my worst nightmare, I desperately wanted to get back to writing. Knox would be out of school soon and I was running out of time. I'd wasted so much of it already. *So much precious time wasted.*

But Tavia continued anyway, "I know, I'm so excited about it! Guess what? This is kind of under wraps right now, but Meryl Streep just signed on to record the audio version of the book! And Reese Witherspoon is featuring it in her book club! AND, you may not believe this, but writers with that much success negotiate multi-million-dollar book deals! So, don't ever let anyone tell you that you can't make money writing. Write your stories, because million-dollar success just may follow. It *does* happen!"

Did she just wink? I looked at her sideways, considering whether or not she had mind reading capabilities. Tavia had no way of knowing that the "anyone" she was referring to, was *me*. I had just been telling *myself* that I couldn't make money writing. And all of a sudden, there she was, telling me I was wrong, refuting my thoughts, as though she'd been reading my mind all along.

She grinned widely at me, "You know, Ann says that the only difference between her and anybody else is that she *takes the time to write*. She says that she believes everyone has a story to tell, but not everyone takes the time to sit down, and to take that story out of their head, and let it flow down their arm," she said, pointing a finger from her shoulder down to her hand, "through their fingertips, and onto the page. It's *all* about taking the time to do it."

I had to keep my mouth from dropping to the floor. I had just been chiding myself for wasting so much time writing and there she was, again, this person I didn't know, reading my mind, and telling me that I was wrong. According to her friend, the multi-millionaire author, it was *all* about taking the time to write.

But what she said next, may have been what hit me the most, square in the middle of my forehead, like an open palm giving me a BOP – a *duh, you idiot!*

"That's why I just love to see people sitting out here doing exactly what you're doing right now. It's what I would be doing if I wasn't at work."

How quickly we forget, when we get the *very* thing that we've longed for, how incredibly special it is. Tavia Cathcart Brown, a beacon of light, came to remind me.

There I was on a weekday, sitting in such a beautiful place in the late morning, the birds chirping, the sun shining, surrounded by nature, doing what I loved to do. How lucky I'd been to not be stuck behind a desk at work crunching numbers, reading regulations, but instead sitting *right* there, in that *very* spot, pursuing my love of writing.

My dream had already come true. And instead of fully embracing and enjoying the moment, I was consumed with my thoughts of the past and the future, in my own personal hell, well on my way to squandering it all away in my mind.

Tavia went on to tell me that she often got to read Ann's books before they were published. Since they had grown up together, Ann always sent her a draft, as she had trusted her to give her honest opinion and feedback along with her team of editors.

When I shared that I was getting to a place where I could really use some honest feedback on my *own* work, she didn't skip a beat in handing me her card.

"Well, I'd be happy to take a look at it for you. Just send it over," Tavia had said in her jolly way, handing over her card, like it was nothing. Like she hadn't just answered my prayers.

Writing is a lonely endeavor. I think that's probably why I like it, because I *am* a bit of a loner. But being on your own with your words day in and day out trying to create something, with no feedback whatsoever, can drive you a little mad. Are you on to something? Or, are you a babbling, raging idiot? One never really knows until others read and weigh in on your madness.

I'd had no resources for honest feedback at the time. No one I knew was a writer and I was too embarrassed to let any of my friends or family read my book, especially not in rough form as it stood. To have a fellow writer read it and let me know if I was on the right track, would mean everything to me.

While Tavia was far too humble to tell me herself during that first encounter, I would later learn that she, too, was an author. She'd published two books on her trade as a nature writer that had sold tens of thousands of copies, one of them winning an award. She'd written articles that had been published in national and regional journals and magazines. She'd also hosted an educational show on television that she'd co-written herself. She was currently in the process of writing her third book, this time a fictional novel.

She was quite possibly the most creative and talented, and *busiest* person I'd ever met, and there she was, offering kindness and inspiration to a stranger, offering her time and expertise to me freely, while she was in the middle of planning her biggest event of the year. It felt as though she was a messenger sent from up above, to remind me how abundant and magical the Universe was, at a time when I *desperately* needed reminding.

After a few emails back and forth, and much stress and deliberation on my part, I finally hit the "send" button on my very rough work. Tavia responded that very same day, telling me how much she loved it. She told me that not only could she not put it down, but that she'd sat in awe of my message afterward. She said she was moved by my stories and that reading my words was nurturing to her soul. She told me that I had a gift for writing and that I should follow through with having my work published as she believed my book would be a success.

Her words brought tears to my eyes. Her kindness was overwhelming. How deeply I had longed to hear those words – to hear that I wasn't wasting my time. To hear that I really had a chance at this, that my dreams weren't in vain.

We would then meet for coffee and Tavia would tell me that I was young and talented and that I had all the time in the world. She would encourage me to keep writing – to keep reaching for my dreams. She would read me some of her work, which was so impressive, my talent paled in her presence. But this served to only reinforce her message to me. If she, with all of her talent, thought that *I* was talented, then perhaps I really was. She gave me the push I needed to keep going when I was so close, right at the precipice, of giving up.

This was the magic I was writing my entire book about. It was coincidental, yet so perfect, so synchronistic and precise, it was as if it were divinely orchestrated. When I asked for help, I received it, in a way that I could have never dreamt up on my own. The perfect person was dropped onto my path, with the clearest of messages, right when I needed it the most. It was like a nod from the Universe.

But *why* I felt my inner four-year-old self ask miserably. If the dreams written on my heart really were meant to be, *why* did it feel like everything was falling apart? Like it was all coming to an end? Was the Universe trying to teach me something? Or better yet, since I am a part of the Universe, what was I trying to teach *myself*?

In that moment, I realized that I had been asking all the wrong questions. I had been asking questions like: *Why me? Why didn't I see this coming? Why didn't I plan better? Why didn't I save more cash? Why did I buy so many things we didn't need? Why did we give such big raises? Why didn't we wait to hire or to build the pool or the outdoor kitchen? Why did I quit my job so hastily? Why did the recession have to hit when it did? Why did taxes have to be so much money?* And on, and on, and on.

But all of these questions were rooted in the events of the past. None of them were focused on the present. And I knew from my studies that thinking that there is something to be done now about an event that occurred in the past only creates suffering in the now.

Since one's mind cannot discern between a thought you keep thinking and an actual event, it is as if you are recreating the event over and over again in the present moment, reliving it, and reinforcing the neural pathways that create your reality.

This was the anxiety that I felt – my body trying to tell me to take action on what my mind was perceiving as happening, when there was no action to be taken, because it had *already* happened. There was nothing to be done about it now. It was in the past, and if I wanted to change the present, if I wanted the anxiety to end, I knew I had to forget the past, and begin creating from the present moment again.

I realized that all of the questions I had been asking myself revolved around one simple thought, phrased in a million different ways: *This shouldn't have happened.*

It was the same thought that had gone round and round in my mind after my sister's accident. And here I was, two and a half years later, finding more reasons to align with this *same* thought, this same neural pathway. I had mourned my sister's death just as I should have in the days and weeks and months following the accident. But even when that mourning period had passed, my body had remained in fight or flight mode. As some would call it, I was a victim of PTSD.

The worst of the worst had happened, and now that I *knew* how easily it could happen, I was in constant fear of it happening *again*. I was reliving the trauma in everyday situations, constantly anticipating that something devastatingly bad would go wrong. Nothing felt like it was solid, nothing felt stable, or steady, or safe.

I was *always* waiting for the other shoe to drop. And then, it did.

While I was in the hospital in May of 2022 giving birth to our daughter, Kyle's father, Rick, was in another hospital across town, after taking a serious fall.

Rick had been diagnosed with prostate cancer several months prior to this, which is typically slow-growing and treatable. He was one of the lucky ones, *so they said,* that was a candidate for radiation beam therapy, which targets the cancer cells and destroys them without having to subject the whole body to all-over radiation or chemotherapy.

We had expected the cancer to be gone when he had his scans after the procedure, or for the cancer cells to at least be shrunken drastically, in need of perhaps another treatment to relinquish them completely. Instead, the scans showed that somehow between the diagnosis and the beam therapy, which was just a few short weeks later, the cancer had spread like wildfire throughout his entire body.

The cancer cells had made their way into several of his major organs and eventually into his bones – and anyone that knows cancer, knows that once it gets into your bones, there is no getting rid of it. Bone cancer is terminal.

Rick was a man that loved life and he was still determined to fight, to live out his remaining years, or possibly months, as long, and as pain-free as possible. He went through a heavy dose of chemo treatments to shrink and reduce the amount of cancer cells in his body, but the chemo side-effects changed him greatly.

Rick became a shell of the man he once was. And as he did, as Kyle watched his father deteriorate, body *and* mind, quicker than we could keep up with, he, too, became a shell of the man *he* once was as well.

Rick being admitted to the hospital after that nasty fall at the exact same time that I was in the hospital giving birth, was just the beginning of Kyle feeling the constant stress and pressure as he tried to reconcile the need to be in three different places at once.

He had a newborn baby, along with a toddler, and a postpartum wife at home. He had a dying father, forty-five minutes across town, becoming increasingly immobile and agitated, and a mother trying to care for him on her own, who was losing her mind in her own right. And finally, a business that was blowing up, without enough manpower to handle it, and employees that relied on him heavily to be able to do their jobs day in and day out.

The anxiety, stress, and sleepless nights got the best of him. He began drinking heavily to cope, and became increasingly difficult to deal with, often taking his anger and frustration out on the one closest to him, *on me.*

There was a definite shift between us when I decided not to go back to work after my maternity leave was up. While Kyle needed me to take on a bigger role in the company, and agreed that it made sense at the time, it only put more pressure on him since he was now the sole provider for our family. And as time passed, he began resenting me for it.

I admit that part of the divide between us took root solely in my mind, as I immediately began feeling the pressure to prove my worth after I'd decided not to go back to work. I had been so convincing about my dream of becoming a *New York Time's Best-Selling Author* that now, I needed to make it happen, and make it happen quick, or else be ousted as a fraud. Gone were the days of writing for the pleasure of it, as I now had something to prove.

Imposter syndrome took over and it created a white knuckled approach to my writing that led to the writer's block I was currently feeling. I began harboring feelings of inadequacy and insecurity. I had gone all in on being a writer, and here I'd sat day after day, questioning myself and my abilities, and unable to write a single word worth reading, while my husband was the epitome of talent and success. I felt inferior to him, unworthy of the money we were making, and of the incredible life we were living.

And these internal feelings began projecting onto my external reality.

While my taking some of the work off Kyle in his business would help him exponentially in the long run, in the short run it was costing him more time and stress to train someone new. With that someone new being *his wife*, you can probably imagine how that dynamic played out. He didn't treat me with respect and patience like he would have a new employee, but instead treated me like his nagging wife who kept constantly reminding him of all the things that needed to be done – things that he simply didn't have the time to do. Of course, I couldn't do anything without him at first. I was not only learning a new system, but an entirely new trade. I had a steep learning curve to work through and it required, by design, that I ask him questions all day long to make sure I was getting it right.

Kyle was overly stressed and covered in work, so he didn't respond well to the constant interruptions. Every time he scoffed at me, blew me off, rushed me to get to the point, got upset over a mistake, or spoke to me in a hateful manner, it served as proof to me of my own unworthiness. The worst part was that my irrational, condescending boss was *my husband*, so I didn't get to just shut it off at 5pm. Add in the drinking, and you can imagine how this difficult dynamic trickled over into our marriage. We quickly found ourselves at a breaking point. We argued in front of the kids, in front of friends, and family, and even his employees. We spent days sometimes not speaking and lost all forms of intimacy.

It was the hardest time in our marriage, and I hate to say that, because we would both tell you that our little girl is the absolute best thing that has ever happened to us, right up there with the blessing of our little boy. But that didn't negate the fact that it was a lot, all at once.

Were we to blame then, for what was happening in our reality now? Our internal state was gruesome and mangled, and full of frustration and anger, fear and loss. It certainly appeared to now be projecting on our external reality. We had many blessings in 2022 that we could have focused on, but instead we had focused on that proverbial spilled coffee, and had let it spread and stain everything around us.

We had let ourselves and each other down by not focusing on the blessings in our lives and the love we had for each other. And now that we were having to cut salaries and fire people, and pull back the financial help we were providing to Kyle's parents who were no longer able to work, we were letting others down as well. With our fall from grace, we were taking so many people we loved down with us.

Our fall from grace. These words struck a chord within me. We *had* fallen from grace, hadn't we? Grace had been responsible for our good luck. Yes, we were the creators of our reality, and we had done our part – we had focused on what we wanted, we had believed it was possible, and we had taken consistent action every day toward our desires – but it was co-creation with the magic that is the Universe, or what some may call God, that had brought so many blessings to us so quickly.

So, the question remained, how do we get back into grace? How could we begin creating intentionally again to our benefit, rather than unintentionally, to our detriment?

Sure, there were things going on around us affecting our emotional state that were seemingly out of our control – my father-in-law's cancer, the recession, taxes, sleepless nights with a crying baby, a booming business that had become all-consuming, construction on our home that seemed to be never-ending and filled with problems – but we had let those things hijack our attention, and we had let the wrong feelings guide us.

We had let our home become a war zone rather than a place of love. Because we felt lousy, we were treating each other lousy, and creating from a place of trauma, of triggers, and reactiveness. We were playing the victim in our own damn stories.

I currently felt the same gripping sickness in my stomach that I'd felt after my sister passed. I felt the same anxiety weighing on my chest, the same racing thoughts, the same hurt and shame and regret, as if I somehow could have, should have, prevented it all from happening, as if I were fully responsible for our life going up in flames. The trauma from my sister's untimely death had been stored in my body and I had inevitably found more reasons to feel all of those emotions all over again.

I had not just lost my sister and was now losing my father-in-law, the Poppy to our children, and one of the greatest men I'd ever known, but felt like I was also losing my husband, which meant losing my family, and now potentially the business, our home, and, least important of course, all of our money.

I realized that my inner state was causing all of these feelings of loss. Logically I knew that I didn't have anything to do with my father-in-law's illness, but it was still helping to show me what I needed to learn. I needed to figure out how to stop this merry-go-round within me, revolving around these feelings of fear, anger, and loss. I needed to *feel* good again and regain control over my emotions. I needed to change what I was seeking. So, I put a new request out into the Universe: *Help me to feel good again.*

Soon after, as I lay in bed during another sleepless night, staring at the ceiling, the heavy feeling of dread sitting on my chest, I picked up my phone to try to get my mind on something else. I came across a meditation called *Manifest While Sleeping* by Amanda Frances. It contained binaural beats, a mash-up of frequencies, that would help put me to sleep, and claimed that the messaging would seep into, and reprogram my subconscious mind while I slept. *Why not*, I'd thought. At this point, anything was worth a try.

This would be the first time I heard this meditation, but I would end up listening to it over and over again, night after night. Her words still echo in my ears to this day:

"I am willing to see this differently. I am willing to perceive this through the mind of God. I am willing to see this through the eyes of love. I am willing to hear this through the voice of truth. I am willing to see this differently… As you change what is going on inside of you, everything you see outside of you will shift as well…"

The meditation seemed to be speaking directly to me, in answer to my silent prayer. And the advice was clear. *A shift in perception*. It's what I wanted for my friend all those years ago, and I could see that it was exactly what I needed now too – to *see things differently*. I removed my focus from the question of *why me*, and began now asking an entirely different one: *How can I see this differently?*

And when I put that potential out into the Universe – that there *was* the potential to see it differently, it made *all* the difference. My mind flooded with truths that I'd been unable to see before. I realized that the business taking a tumble and our finances going up in flames was not the problem, it was simply a symptom of the bigger problem that had lay beneath the surface. And this symptom had in fact served us. It had halted us right in our tracks. We had been barreling ahead along a timeline, not of our intentional choosing, without paying one bit of attention to where we were headed.

But now? Now we had no choice but to stop, to look around, and to wonder how we'd gotten here, where we had gone wrong. We had no choice but to course correct in a major way. Perhaps best of all, we had no choice but to communicate with and to lean on one another for support – to work through it together, which was something we desperately needed at the time.

We had a unique opportunity before everything turned to ash, to be reminded of what was really important. The situation had checked both mine, and my husband's, egos. And it had lifted the veil on all the silly things we had gotten so caught up in.

Our resulting situation reminded me of a quote I'd always loved, "Before great change comes great chaos." Chaos is so often the catalyst for change as it shows you that things are no longer working. Everything must fall apart to be rebuilt anew. We needed a stronger foundation to build upon.

While Kyle and I had thought we had mastered our thoughts, beliefs, and actions, it seemed we had perhaps missed the most important part of the equation, the part that everything else relied upon, the part that everything is influenced, even perhaps dictated by: *Our feelings*.

I realized that I hadn't felt good in a long time, yet had carried on, ignoring those feelings. But *now*? I could no longer ignore them. They had made themselves blatantly clear – the weight on my chest, the emptiness in the pit of my stomach, the racing of my heart, and the shake in my hands – my body was now *screaming* at me to pay attention, to *listen*.

I thought a lot about my relationship with my husband and how bad it had gotten. He was the love of my life, there was no mistaking or questioning that. Nothing made me feel as good as he did. And nothing made me feel worse than being at odds with him or to consider my life without him.

No, he did not handle stress well. And yes, he unfairly took his stress out on me. This was a character trait that was difficult for me to deal with. But he was going through the toughest time in his life, losing his father. And he, too, was dealing with the change and stress of a newborn baby, no doubt having his own experience, even if it seemed he was oblivious to mine.

Expecting Kyle to be without flaw, when he did so many things exceptionally well, was irrational. I certainly had plenty of flaws, myself, and he had to deal with *those*. This was just one area that he needed additional support, he needed to learn and grow, and I needed to help him do that. Punishing him was not the way. I needed to be the example for him. I needed to begin treating him how I desired him to treat me.

The truth was, he was a great dad and a great husband, just like he was a great son and a great boss. He was incredible, and he was mine. And for that, I needed to be thankful. Focusing on all the ways he had failed or faltered did not serve me, it only created more of what I didn't want. And it certainly didn't *feel good* to be at war with my husband, to have these hateful thoughts about him. Love *felt* much better.

I decided to lean into that feeling. I knew I needed to show my appreciation for him, to say these things out loud, and to stop the incessant narrative in my head about how terrible he was.

And so, I did. Just like that, I made the decision, and I changed. I put my blinders up and focused only on what I loved about him. Every time I found myself going round and round in my head about something he'd said or did and found myself feeling disappointed or angry, I caught it, and course-corrected my thoughts, focusing instead on the feeling of love that I had for him. It was surprisingly easy to just lean into those feelings instead.

And pretty soon, Kyle started reciprocating the feeling of love and mirroring back my thoughts and behaviors.

I took a hard look at the areas of my life where I felt discontented. I loved my kids more than anything in the world, but I felt run-down by all of the responsibility – the day after day of drop offs and pick-ups, feedings and diaper changes, lunch and dinners, dishes and cleanup, bathtimes and bedtime routines. There was always something that needed to be done, and the majority of it all had inevitably fallen on my shoulders once I'd quit my job.

I realized that I needed to find a way to start enjoying my role as a mother again. I had an incredible life, one that I had always dreamed of, and if I couldn't find happiness now, then I would *never* find it. I got intentional about looking for joy in the everyday moments.

I sat down and made a list of everything I loved and everything that brought me joy, both big and small, and brainstormed ways I could incorporate those things into my life more. I restructured my days and weeks in ways that felt good to me, focusing on my energy and alignment first, and finding ways to make even the mundane more enjoyable. I re-envisioned my life, daydreamed on how I could find more joy in my days, and imagined a different me, a wife and a mother that wasn't run down, full of stress, and living in chaos, but one that was joyful and happy, and fun-loving. I started focusing on myself again and taking the time I needed to regain my sanity.

It was difficult at first, the looks I was on the receiving end of, the conversations forced. But momentum was being created. And soon, it became easier. Soon, I was creating from a place of joy again. My joy seemed to spill over and bring my entire family joy as well. I felt like I was being a better mother, wife, business partner, aunt, daughter – all of it. Our home was again filled with love, and Kyle was looking at me in a completely different way, perhaps because I wasn't scowling all the time.

Quicker than I could have ever anticipated, the inward shift toward feeling good started shifting our external reality as well. The business picked back up and we started making a profit again. A financial advisor we could trust, along with a tax strategist, and a bookkeeper, fell right into our laps in the most synchronistic way possible.

It wasn't until I handed all of our financial information over to them to manage, that I breathed a sigh of relief, that I realized how much pressure I had felt doing it all myself. They provided us with a plan of action to get ourselves out of the hole we were in, and to make sure we never found ourselves there again. If we followed their advice, depending on how well the market performed, we'd be sitting on somewhere between $28 - $270 million dollars in assets by the time we retired. We weren't just going to keep our home, but we would still be millionaires after all – *multi-millionaires*.

While this had always been our desire, we had not initially been prepared for that kind of money. We hadn't made the space for it. There was nowhere to put it, which is likely why we spent so much of it! We didn't understand taxes or how to spend money in a favorable way so that we didn't owe as much. We simply weren't ready.

But now, we were. Before our financial trouble, we didn't know what we didn't know. But now, we *knew* we didn't know it. And we finally had the right people in place who did, the right accounts, and the right protections.

Polarity creates clarity. The Universe had taught us what we needed to know to realize our dreams in the most direct and efficient manner possible. These lessons were not easy to learn, and I'd venture to bet that they never are. Unfortunately, for many people, this is the moment they give up and accept defeat. But we didn't.

We didn't give up. We didn't accept failure. We didn't get divorced. We didn't lose our family, or our home, or the business. We reviewed and reassessed our methods, and tried again. We re-envisioned our lives, rebuilding the foundation stronger than it was before. And we thrived. We realized our hopes and dreams and appreciated it all the more, *because* we almost lost it all, *because* we experienced hardship, *because* we experienced tragedy.

And now, I finally knew how to finish the final chapter of my book. I knew I was finally ready to finish telling our story.

I am ready to complete the final manifestation on my list and become the author I've always dreamed of becoming. Will there still be set-backs and failures? I'm certain of it.

It may not be this book, it may not be the next book, or even the one after that. But it *will* happen. I *will* become a *New York Times Best Selling Author*.

I *know* it, because it's been the dream on my heart since I was a little girl. I *know*, because I've **thought** about it every single day for as long as I can remember. I *know*, because I'm saying the **thought** out loud, just as I did with my thought about becoming a millionaire.

I· *know*, because I seek out the proof of it and **believe** in its possibility. I *know*, because I **believe** it deep down in my soul, not just that I can do it, but that I was *made* to do it, and that in some version of reality that I'm choosing to tune into now, I truly **believe** that I've *already* done it.

I *know*, because it **feels** good to write and because I already **feel** the emotions of being the best-selling author now. I *know*, because it **feels** good to take the steps every day to align with her. I *know*, because I **feel** just as good during the journey as I imagine the destination will feel.

I *know* I will do it, because I won't stop taking **action** on this dream of mine. I'll keep taking one inspired **action** after another toward my goal each and every day until it happens, no matter how incremental, even if it takes me until I'm 90 years old.

But I bet it won't take that long. Because while it could take little old me another fifty years of practice, and learning, and set-backs, and failures, it's *not* just little old me.

I'm a part of something *much* bigger. Something that shows me what I need to do next and provides me with an infinite number of resources to help me do it. Something that I can put all of my faith in, that I can be sure of, as long as I keep listening to the voice within and doing my part to make it happen.

And *that* – the doing my part – is something I have complete and total control over. *I* am fully in control of my life. And there is no other way that I would want it to be.

> *"I'll teach you how to jump on the wind's back, and then away we go."*
>
> PETER PAN

Rick (Poppy) Littrell with his grandchildren, Khloe & Knox

LESSONS ON FLOW

"Once you make a decision, the Universe conspires to
make it happen."

RALPH WALDO EMERSON

The Psychology of Flow

The term "flow" was first coined by a psychologist by the name of Mihaly Csikszentmihalyi in the 1960's. He discovered a cognitive state that is entered into when one is fully absorbed in an activity, often one that is challenging, but also enjoyable.

Commonly referred to as being "in the zone", it is when you are so immersed in what you are doing, it seems as though time stands still, and you are completely unaware of everything else going on around you. It is the experience of Kairos time, as discussed in the last section.

This heightened, focused state often gives way to optimal knowledge, creativity, performance, and results with, what would seem to be, very little effort. It is called flow because it is as though one is being carried along by a current in a flowing stream of water. Knowledge, ability, and creativity flows through you, as if it is channeled or downloaded from somewhere other than the conscious mind.

We *know* it does not come from the mind, because neuropsychology studies have shown a significant decrease in the brain's activity while in this flow state. The brain appears to shut down, which is the opposite of what you would expect, since it is also when people are at their best, when their true genius is being fully expressed. As according to Steven Kotler, an expert who has studied flow for decades says, "Flow is the telephone booth where Clark Kent changes clothes, the place from where Superman emerges."

Michael Jordan, who is widely accepted as the greatest basketball player of all time, is known for the incredible, almost superhuman things he did on the court throughout his career. He holds the record for the highest vertical jump in the world and people often say he didn't jump, he flew. He did things during games that would seem impossible, such as making shots with his eyes closed or shooting with his non-dominant hand. Even though he was known for being a mediocre three-point shooter, during one game, he shot a series of six three-pointers in a row, only to shrug his shoulders at the camera afterward as if he, himself, didn't know where the ability came from.

Michael Jordan, whether he realized it at the time or not, was shutting down his mind and tapping into flow. If Jordan was thinking with his rational mind, he probably wouldn't have started those jumps from so far away from the basket. He probably wouldn't have taken such a huge chance by closing his eyes or putting the ball in his non-dominant hand when shooting during an important game. If he was thinking about his less-than-stellar skill at shooting three-pointers, he probably wouldn't have taken such a huge chance on that fourth, fifth, or sixth shot. Given that the odds were against him, *based on his ability*, he likely would have decided to safely pass the ball instead. But Jordan wasn't making those decisions using his conscious mind, he was *feeling* into his next move.

Michael Jordan did not find greatness through his rational mind. He found it through flow, in allowing himself to get lost in doing what he loved to do. And by allowing his body to take over, and his intuition to guide him, he became the greatest basketball player of all time.

Successful athletes, artists, musicians, writers, actors, and other creatives are all very aware of flow. They spend their lives trying to perfect their process for *tapping in* to flow. They know that this is where their genius lies. It is where they find their full potential and unlimited talent. And, perhaps most importantly, it's where they find the most *joy*.

It is a place where they are subject to no fear, no hesitation, and no worry. They are not thinking about the past or the future. They are not focused on the outcome, but focused in the moment. While in this state, there is no thinking, there is only *feeling*. And through feeling, rather than thinking, one is able to create God-like results.

The Universe Flows with You

The word flow has many definitions in the dictionary, but the one I find most interesting, from the Merriam Webster dictionary is "to derive from a source".

As we've already discussed, what you call this "source" is entirely up to you. But know that it is the *source of everything*, of *all that is*. It is this source flowing through you, in co-creation, that generates this enhanced creative state that produces such optimal results.

If you've ever taken any kind of psychedelic drug, you have likely experienced a fairly accurate visual representation of flow. While it is said that these drugs create hallucinations, I believe what they actually do is lift the veil momentarily, allowing one to see what typically cannot be seen by the human eye.

Often, what results is one's inner world projected externally. This is why some people have the most beautiful, breakthrough experiences on these drugs while others may have, what one might call, a "bad trip". Their inner emotional state is creating their perception of their external reality. I believe with or without drugs, this is always occurring – our internal world projecting outward. But the drugs magnify it in an almost cartoonish way, one that cannot be ignored, to show you first-hand what is going on inside of you.

While under the spell of psychedelics, there are common visuals that people report seeing. The whole world appears as though it's come alive – both living, and inanimate objects, the same. Trees and houses, cars and grass – it all seems to be moving together in tandem, in a cohesive back and forth rhythm, swaying along to a symphony that only they seem to hear. It's as if you can actually *see* quantum energy moving through everything.

There is also a common feeling reported of a connectedness to it all, a deep feeling of oneness. One becomes aware that they are both significant and insignificant, everything and nothing, all at once, as though you are nothing more but the mere subatomic particles you are made up of, the same subatomic particles that create everything around you. You are no more or less than the tree and the house, or the grass and the car. You are simply a part of the whole. And when you flow with the whole, when you vibrate right along with it, you become one with it. You tap into the rhythm of it all and you *become* the whole.

A countless number of people have been known to have significant breakthroughs, heal severe traumas and mental illness, and some even claim to learn the meaning of life through these experiences. The body *feels*, rather than *thinks*, and it *heals*. The Universe provides the medicine.

I'm not advocating that you try psychedelic drugs, as a matter of fact I would say to be very careful if you choose to do so, as the people you are with, the environment you are in, as well as your mental state at the time, and certainly the dosage you take, has a great impact on your experience. My intention is only that you use the feelings and visuals that I've described to you above to envision everything in the Universe alive, connected, and working together in a cohesive dance. When you find flow, you become one with this rhythm, you lock into it, and the entire world flows right along with you.

This is how coincidences, synchronicities, serendipities, and miracles occur. The Universe moves to meet you, to envelope you in its rhythm, to sway you in the direction of the most optimal path forward for you, and for all.

I believe this is how we are supposed to experience life – not separate, not disrupting and pushing against nature, not in conflict within ourselves and with those around us, but in a cohesive dance, working together. The only true scenario in which one wins, is a scenario in which all win. In business this is known as a win-win situation and is typically the only way in which any kind of partnership thrives.

It is also the secret to life. What's good for the micro is good for the macro, and vice versa. As below, so above, and as within, so without. Everything is designed to flow together. What is best for you is never contradictory to nature, and as such, will never produce contradictory feelings within. The path that is best for you produces only joy. It will *feel* good to follow it, and it will never be at the detriment of someone else.

With every step you take in life, flow is right there within arms-length, ready to scoop you up and place you into the path of the current, the steady stream of infinite knowledge and potential. But admittedly, the current can be elusive if you don't know how to find it.

Finding Flow

People often find themselves in a state of flow purely by accident.

One might find flow while involved in an activity they enjoy that allows their body to take over such as swimming or surfing, dancing, or playing an instrument or a sport. They may find that they become one with the activity, their tool, or gear, or instrument becoming an extension of their own body, as they seamlessly move into the perfect positions at the exact right moments.

One might find it while participating in creative outlets, such as painting, writing, singing, or playing the guitar. They may find that what flows out of them in these moments is beautiful, poetic and profound, as if it is flowing *through* them rather than being produced *by* them.

Some might find it during intentional practices that slow down the mind, such as meditation, breathwork, walking in nature, yoga, or tai-chi. They may find that brilliant ideas or answers come to them out of nowhere, or perhaps even later throughout the day as they maintain the peaceful state they tapped into. Many professional athletes, artists, and actors will use these practices before participating in their craft to get themselves into a flow state before they begin. Some do them on a daily or regular basis to prime their minds and bodies for flow each day.

The moment that one realizes they are in flow, however, and starts to think about it, is often the same moment it starts drifting away from them. One's brain takes over and begins to question what is happening. Doubt creeps into the mind as they begin to wonder how long they can continue in this enhanced state, downloading information, or creating, or performing, or producing at the pace, or accuracy, or joy that they are currently witnessing. The mind starts forcing, rather than allowing, and there is a resulting pressure that seems to override the pleasure. The flow stops.

Imagine yourself in a boat being pulled steadily along by the current, but then you start paddling. And because you cannot *see* the current, cannot figure out where it is using your mind, you are paddling in the wrong direction, eventually paddling yourself right out of the current! Forcefully paddling like this may still get you where you are going eventually, but it will not come easily, it will not come quickly, it will not feel joyful. It will feel like you are paddling upstream, fighting against the current.

This is the epitome of hustle culture and it is what we are taught from a young age – that being busy is like a badge of honor, that working hard and being extremely productive is the way to success. However, this is not the most direct route to success. Like water that always finds the path of least resistance, you are designed to do the same.

The most direct route to success is intuitively taking action only when the timing is right, when you feel the nudge, when the spark of inspiration hits. It is allowing, rather than forcing. It is in finding joy in the journey, not forging ahead expecting the joy to come only as a result of reaching your destination.

Once flow has been experienced, one knows that it *is* the ultimate goal. After realizing the potential within and the euphoria that these moments of being pulled along the current bring, people will wonder, often to no avail, where it came from, why it left, and how to find it again. The problem with this is that flow is not found in the rational mind.

Once again, I call your attention to Albert Einstein's quote, "I think 99 times and find nothing. I stop thinking, swim in silence, and the truth comes to me...I didn't arrive at my understanding of the fundamental laws of the Universe through my rational mind." This, from the man most known for his brain.

To find flow, one must shut down their rational mind and get lost in the feeling of joy instead. While the activities mentioned above can certainly put you into a state of joyous flow, my offering to you is that flow can actually be a way of life, not just something that happens every-once-in-a-while during particular activities. It can be found in the small, simple joys of the everyday.

You can remain in a state of flow, certainly drifting in and out with the ebbs and flows of the day, but it can become your default state, the state of being that you consistently return to time and time again, with ease.

Can you imagine how amazing this would be? To ooze creativity, and imagination, and intelligence, to attract at maximum potential, and to feel happy, and connected, and joyful all the time, no matter what one is doing? Just as flow allows you to create with ease, you can also get into a state of flow with ease as well.

A Child-Like Sense of Wonder

When we come into this world, we have no concept of time. An hour, later this evening, last week, tomorrow, a month from now, a year from now, it all means nothing to a child.

My five-year-old son asks blankly, "but what does that *mean*? But *when* is it? *When* is the sleepover, *when* is Halloween, *when* will Nana and Papaw be here?"

We talk in terms of Peppa the Pig episodes and the length of a Paw Patrol Movie. We talk in terms of before or after meal and snack times, and how many sleeps. Three sleeps and Nana and Papaw will be here. "Ah, ok!" he says. And then an hour later, "how many sleeps *now* until Nana and Papaw will be here?"

You see, time means nothing to him. It is a foreign concept much like a foreign language may be to us. It has no rhyme or reason, no relativity to anything in his world.

After all, he doesn't really want to know *when*. He wants to know when it is *now*. Because *now* is all that exists to a child.

Hard at play, children aren't thinking about all the things that have been done or need to be done, other people's expectations of them, or their opinions about what they are, or are not, doing. They aren't thinking about that nasty fall they took thirty seconds ago or the inevitable lashing to come when their mom sees the mess they've made.

They aren't thinking of any particular regrets or consequences because they have no concept of the past or the future. The future is not real, not yet anyway, and nothing is dealt with in a child's mind before being right there in front of them, in that moment. And then, it's on to the next moment.

I saw this so clearly after my sister passed. Her daughter, Kylie, at five-years-old, wanted her mommy. And then, in the next moment, she wanted to play. Kylie had no concept of time, of past or future. She didn't know to mourn for what she would be missing out on in the coming days, and weeks, and years, and even decades ahead, without her mother there by her side, without her mother just a phone call away.

Kylie couldn't consider how lucky she'd been in the past to have a mother that doted over her the way Dana had. To think back to all the mother-daughter shopping trips, or perfectly themed, over-the-top birthday parties, or the cute dresses and bows atop sweetly curled hair, and think that was then, and no longer now.

I think about *my* mother. I think about the way the whole room lights up when she enters, the feeling of home when her arms wrap around me, the immediate relief I feel when I've told her my troubles. I think about her care and concern over me, her devotion and commitment to helping me through all of life's challenges. How she'll gobble up each and every one of my problems, big or small, and take them upon herself, as if they were her own. How she relieves me of my worries and finds solutions when I don't have the time, or resources, or knowledge to do so myself. I think about her love, unconditional, and as sure as the sun is to shine, and the way that she makes everything better, just by being there. And I think, there is *nothing* like a mother's love. It is perhaps the greatest gift that life has to give. And I have to assume that when it is taken away, there is a void that can never be filled.

But for Kylie, she knew none of this. She still had her child-like sense of wonder to lean on. She had no concept of time, of past or future, no fear or anxiety over what was to come. She didn't know what was to come and that was perfectly fine with her. She didn't need to know. Because the ever present now was not a time to be lost in the past or the future. It was simply a great time to play.

And in the same way that Caleb, at less than a year old, would stick out his neck and tilt his head to the side, so that only one big, round eye was looking right at you, and grin as big and as a wide and as goofy as possible, just to get a surprised chuckle out of you, Dana's children showed us every day what it meant to be alive.

It meant living in the now. Not just living in the now, but living *for* the now, living for *joy* in the now. Looking for joy around every corner, creating joy even when there is none around the corner, being fully present to the magic swirling around you and always, *always* being ready to create more of that magic.

This was likely your experience as a child as well. It's who you came into the world being, before you were molded and shaped into something else entirely. Before all the noise took over and you found yourself spending more time lost in your head, in the past and in the future and in other people's perceptions and expectations of you, rather than living in the joyous moment of now.

As a child, you allowed creativity to flow, uninhibited. You weren't thinking of any specific outcome as you were stacking blocks or connecting magnets, yet still, you immersed yourself in the activity, and delighted in surprise at the glorious final product when you felt you were done.

You created, built, destroyed, rebuilt, and destroyed again. You felt no lasting attachment to your creations as they served their purpose of being fun to make and to admire in the moment. You did not dwell on what could have been, should have been, when your creation got knocked over by the dog or your little sister. You felt the emotions in the moment and let them out, pouted or cried, or threw a fit, and then, it was on to the next moment, forgotten entirely.

You simply did what felt good, and then what felt good to do next. You did what came naturally to you – you played. You felt pulled toward activities that you had a natural ability in, things that were both fun and challenging for you. And through this play, you practiced, you learned, you gained knowledge, and you improved your skills and your talents.

There is a reason why children can learn a foreign language far quicker than we can, because they are fully in the moment of learning, fully open without thoughts of the past or future clouding their mind, without expectation of time or difficulty, and completely and utterly detached from the result.

This is flow. It is being completely immersed in the now, allowing your intuition to guide you from point A to point B, from one spark of joy to the next, without your mind getting in the way. It is *feeling* into your next move, based on what *feels good*, rather than thinking into it, based on what you *think* you should do.

Internal Guidance System

What you innately knew as a small child is what I'd like you to re-learn now. Feeling good is of the upmost importance. Feeling good right now, not later when you finish the work day, not a couple weeks from now when you go on vacation, not in two years from now when you finish school, or make partner, or have a child, not when you retire, but *now*.

When you feel good, you find more and more reasons to feel good. Your life gets better and better. You become magnetic, pulling more people, places, ideas, and things toward you that create more good feelings.

And it was meant to be this way, this is how you were designed. Your feelings are like your internal guidance system, pulling you in one direction and away from another, indicating what is right for you and what is wrong for you. When something feels good to do or to have done, it is right for you. When it feels bad to do or to have done, it is wrong for you.

You may be thinking, *but it can't be that easy*. After all, what if what feels good to you is lying in bed all day, eating potato chips, and watching television? While that feels good to do, it surely can't be what's best for you, or the world, or lead to creating the life of your dreams, *right?*

Actually, it can. Sure, overconsumption does typically make us feel bad – emphasis on the *feeling bad* – when you do it too often. But in moderation, it can actually be incredibly helpful. So often we ignore our urges for rest or pleasure because we've been conditioned to believe it is "bad" to follow these urges. We think we need to be "on" all the time and glorify working around the clock and being in a constant state of busy, as if that is the only way to success. When in reality, rest and pleasure can be the quickest way to quantum leap your life forward.

Remember, when you're in the current, paddling is unnecessary. You can lie back, relax, and enjoy the steady movement forward. You can decide to pick up the paddle only when it feels good to do so, and know that regardless, you are headed in the right direction.

When you are not in the current the best thing you can do is stop struggling. Stop pushing against the current and lie back, feel the motion of the water, get in tune with the water, let the water lead you. Let your body lead you.

If your desire is to lie in bed and watch television all day, it is an indication that you are not in the current. You are likely paddling forcefully. And in order for you to find the current again, your mind and body need to take a break from the paddling.

People often come back from vacation renewed and ready to take on their work again with a new sense of vigor and purpose. This is because they were fully living in the moment, feeling good, while playing and resting on vacation. People so often experience downloads of new ideas and answers to problems they have been struggling with, while taking time away from their work to relax and enjoy life. Upon return, work often seems to be joyful again.

People who return from vacation more tired than they left typically were not living in the moment. They were dreading their return, focused on the temporary nature of their vacation, mentally already back at work, anticipating the work to be piled high upon their return.

Writers receive the advice that if you are feeling stuck and the words are not flowing, to get up and move – to take a walk or go do something fun, to go out and experience life. Once they return to their desk, the words often magically start flowing again.

When one is constantly busy, there is no room for intuitive downloads to come through. Energy is constantly being depleted rather than being restored. So many people ignore their internal guidance system. I venture to say that this is why so many people are getting sick and dealing with often invisible, chronic illnesses, and even disease. It's a major reason why stress, anxiety, and depression are so prevalent. Your body is *always* speaking to you.

When physical ailments arise in your body, it is your internal guidance system telling you that you have veered off course and you have spent too long ignoring the subtle nudges to course correct. You have spent too long denying your feelings of unhappiness and doing nothing to change them. Rather than taking action to change your feelings, you have allowed the bad feelings to continue to compound. What begins as negative emotions turns into pain, discomfort, and disease (as in, not at ease) in the body. This is your body's way of screaming at you when all of the intuitive whispers have gone unanswered.

Science now tells us that stress is the leading cause of chronic illnesses. But stress is a natural body reaction, and is actually a positive thing, as it can help you to avoid danger, or meet a deadline, or prompt you to change your life if needed. It is a call to action. Your body's response to stress is to release hormones that increase your heart and breathing rates and ready your muscles to respond. So, if you are in a life-or-death situation, it is especially important, as it prepares you for fight or flight.

The problem, however, is that fight or flight weakens your immune system as all functions that are not critical to survival essentially shut down, creating damaging effects throughout your entire body. Parts of your brain shut down as well, including the prefrontal cortex, which makes you unable to utilize problem-solving skills or creative thinking. And now, what was meant to occur only in short bursts, is taking over people's lives, becoming their default state of being, as many *stay* in a chronic state of stress. Why?

In 1936, the term stress was defined, in its biological connotation, as "the non-specific response of the body to any demand for change." The question becomes, then, why is our body perceiving a constant demand for change? And why aren't we listening to this demand and working through, or removing, the stressors?

Our bodies are screaming at us and we are oblivious to it. We take a pill for this symptom or that symptom, and we refuse to look at the root cause. We are not living our lives in alignment, based on how we want to feel in the moment, but instead living our lives for the past and the future, based on past hurts and regrets and future fears and anxieties.

As those neural pathways in our brains are cemented into place with the same repetitive thoughts and actions day after day, pretty soon we are simply going through the motions as if in a trance, not even thinking about what we are doing or why. We simply find ourselves a part of the matrix – working ourselves to death to fund an overreaching and yet, highly incompetent government, to participate in out-of-control consumerism to buy things we don't need or want in an attempt to fill the void, and throwing the rest of our money into a broken healthcare system, trying to reverse what we, ourselves, have created, and what simply *cannot* be reversed through medicine.

More Americans than ever are experiencing chronic anxiety. My advice to you if you are experiencing anxiety on a regular basis is to take a good hard look at your life. You are likely spending your time doing things that don't feel good, doing things only for other people, or for what you believe to be a necessity, rather than following your feelings, your intuition, and the hits of inspiration that come all day long. There is likely something within you that has been pulling at you to do, and you have likely been ignoring it. You push it all back down because you do not have the time, nor the bandwidth, to deal with it.

I remind you, however, that true satisfaction can only be found in having a desire and moving in the direction of that desire. Nothing else will bring your life purpose, fulfillment, and happiness, like this will. And until you can make this switch, expect the anxiety to compound until it eventually takes over your entire life, giving you no choice but to pay attention to it. Remember though, all of this can be reversed. All can be saved in a single moment when you decide to start following your heart.

Your urge, then, to lie in bed and watch television all day, is really just your body's way of telling you it is time to slow down, time to take a break. I cannot begin to count how many times I have had this urge and have pushed it down, trudging ahead, only to find myself soon in bed, not by choice, but due to sickness, within a short amount of time after having ignored it.

If you are honest with yourself, while your desire in this moment very well could be to lie in bed watching television all day, that is not your deepest desire, day after day, for an entire lifetime. Feeling good can only come in short bursts from these kinds of desires. While it may feel good to do every once in a while, you have desires that far exceed this. But, if you haven't met your most basic desires for rest, just as Maslow's Hierarchy of Needs Pyramid shows, you cannot focus on any of your bigger desires until that most basic need is met.

Often, after a day or so of lying in bed, you will feel re-energized. It is then that you will feel the intense motivation to get up and move with vigor and enthusiasm. If vigor and enthusiasm do not come after a day or two of rest, it is because you have nothing to look forward to in getting up to move – you are dreading what you have to do. Your body is speaking. Listen to it. Find something you love to do. Even a small part of your day spent on doing something you love will change your life.

People have a hard time trusting their feelings because they have gotten into the practice of denying themselves their desires for so long, that they eventually binge on those desires later in a very unhealthy way. And once momentum is gained, it can be difficult to break the cycle of over-extending and then over-consuming. It becomes habitual, a part of who you are that is no longer a conscious choice.

At the root of it all, your emotions and feelings are, by design, your body's way of signaling to you that it is time to take some sort of action for the betterment of yourself. And when you deny yourself that action, you deplete your resources and inhibit your own growth.

If you were to lie in bed, eating potato chips, and watching television day after day, after day, you would become extremely uncomfortable and unhappy. That is your body's way of telling you it's time to now get up and move.

When you put your hand in fire, you feel pain. That feeling is designed to make you remove your hand from the fire. When you experience hunger pains, it is your body's way of motivating you to get up and cook yourself something to eat. When you eat a fresh, juicy piece of fruit and feel pleasure, that feeling is designed to make you want to seek out the nutrients your body needs to thrive. When you feel full, it is your body's way of telling you you've had an adequate amount of food. When you eat two pieces of cake and you feel like you want to throw up, that is your body's way of telling you not to do that again. When you feel lazy, it is your body's way of telling you it's time to rest or to find something that you can be excited about.

When you feel dread and anxiety on Sunday night because you know you have to go to work the next morning, that feeling is designed to make you quit that job that brings you so much unhappiness. When you think about your dream job, or your passion project, your body fills with excitement. That feeling is designed to make you take action to pursue that dream.

Start paying attention to your feelings, as they are, by design, a call to action. Let them guide you. Start doing more of what brings you joy and stop doing the things that make you feel bad. Let your Internal Guidance System lead you from moment to moment. As hits of inspiration come, and your body fills with excitement at the thought, follow the spark.

There are times, however, when your feelings are not about what you are experiencing in the present moment. What if, like me, when I was thinking over and over again, *this shouldn't have happened*, you are lost in the past and experiencing negative feelings based on something that there is nothing you can do about now? How do you regain control of your mind and your emotions, and find your way back into the present moment again? How do you get back into the now, and thus, back into flow?

The Perfect Storm

I mentioned earlier that our financial crisis was the result of one questionable decision upon another, which had fallen in line with a cruel act of the economy – the recession, which had effectively created the perfect storm for us.

My sister's accident was a perfect storm as well. So many things had to align, ever so perfectly, in order for it to have happened. A slight variation in any one of a laundry list of moments, and Dana would likely still be here today. This was one of the things that drove Shawn crazy afterward – the *what ifs* – going over the timeline, again, and again.

What if they had not made the crazy decision to go straight from vacation to the lake house to join in on the Halloween festivities that weekend? What if he had not gone out on the ATV earlier and hadn't even seen the lake being dug? What if he hadn't mentioned it while they were sitting around the campfire? What if he hadn't said to Dana, who gave him a look when he suggested it, "Cameron can keep an eye on the kids, come with us." What if he had thought to check to see if everyone had their seatbelts on before he started driving? What if he had not taken that exact route, or not gone up that damn hill so slowly? What if the dirt at the top hadn't been laid fresh that day? What if they would have gone to look at it the next night, after the rain had matted it down? What if he had reached out and tried to grab her when they started to tilt?

It shouldn't have happened. Yet, it did.

And the fact that it did, was no more Shawn's fault than our financial problems were mine. We didn't know what we didn't know, we acted and reacted only as we could have in each and every moment, and that, combined with the only way those around us could have acted and reacted, along with external conditions aligning just as they did, created the perfect storm. And it could have been no other way. As Albert Einstein once famously said, "God does not play dice with the Universe."

Everything happens for a reason. I used to hate this saying. My sister didn't *die for a reason.* It was senseless. I don't believe God needed another angel more than my niece and nephew needed a mother. She should still be here with us today, holding her babies. There was a time when I wanted to tell anyone who said such a thing to *fuck off.* But the truth is, much like everything else in our world, it is all about perception. There is polarity and duality in everything, including token phrases and beliefs such as these.

It wasn't until I heard a Rapid Resolution Therapist, Andrea Crowder, on a podcast one day, explain it in terms of the perfect storm that I really got it. She used the example of a perfect storm to help someone resolve their feelings of hurt toward their mother for something that had happened in the past.

To do this, she told a story about a little boy whose tree swing in his back yard had fallen to the ground during a storm. The little boy, who was incredibly upset, kept saying to his mother, "Why did this happen? *This shouldn't have happened!*" The boy's mother tried to tell him that nothing could be done now about the swing, but the little boy wouldn't accept this and just became more hysterical, continuing to cry and say, "*This shouldn't have happened!*"

The mother then decided to take a different approach. She asked the boy to consider what he'd been learning in school about math and science and to recall the law of cause and effect. She asked him if one plus one always equals two, and what happens when one pushes a light switch down.

The mother then goes on to explain that there was a terrible storm the night before that involved very heavy rains, and strong winds, and a very old tree with an extremely unhealthy, weak branch that hadn't had any growth on it for years. She asked the boy to consider the exact weight of the rain and the exact speed of the winds, the exact age of the tree, and the weakness of the branch, as well as the laws of gravity and cause and effect.

She explained to the boy that all of this had come together to create an exact equation. She asked the boy to consider, based on this exact equation, if the tree branch could have fallen three inches to the left. She tells him to remember math and science and the very *specific* numbers at play – does one plus one always equal two? Yes, of course.

Math and science tell us that the branch had to have fallen right where it did, in that very spot, as that was the exact answer to an exact equation. She then asked the boy, could the branch have not fallen at all? Of course not, it *had* to fall, there could be no other way. And if it *had* to fall just as it did, could you now go back and make it *not* fall? No, of course not. It had to happen, just as it did. It was an exact equation.

While we can often apply science and math to things such as these, we don't readily apply it to ourselves or to others. We are all made up of an exact equation of numerous factors, many outside of our control – genetics, DNA, environment, economic, socio, political, and religious backgrounds, belief systems we were born into, past experiences and traumas, etc.

And when you take all of that and then add in other people's factors, as well as the changing external conditions such as weather, time of day or year, the economy, technology, etc., what you get is an equation, an equation that can only have one answer.

The Rapid Resolution Therapist, who again, was helping someone to get over a past hurt involving their mother, came back to the question, "So, could your mother have reacted any differently than she did in that moment? Could the branch have fallen three inches to the left? Could it have not fallen at all? The answer is always NO. Science. Math. Now, could it have happened any differently *now*? Can you stop it from happening? Can you go back to this morning and not put those shoes on that you are wearing? No, you can't. *It doesn't exist.*"

She goes on to tell a story about a baby being rescued from a burning house. The man that saved the baby was being interviewed by the news. When asked what made him run into the burning house, he says "I don't know. I saw the house was burning. I heard the baby crying. I didn't think. I just ran in."

Other spectators, all good people, stood frozen in fear, staring at the fire and listening to the baby cry. They didn't run into the house. *Why?*

The mother left the baby at home alone to walk down the street to go buy a pack of cigarettes. *Why* did she leave her baby home alone? *Why* did she need a cigarette so badly right then?

A man came walking by the house and overheard the woman as she was walking out, talking to her friend on the phone, saying she would only be gone for a few minutes and the baby would be fine. She just *had* to have a cigarette before she lost it. And the man thinks, *I'm going to teach this woman a lesson.* He then sets the house on fire. *Why* would he set a house on fire with a baby in it?

A hero, cowards, an addict, an arsonist. Who is right and who is wrong? Who should have, could have, acted differently?

As the Stoic philosopher, Epictetus stated, "It is not events that disturb people, it is their judgements concerning them." It simply is not about right or wrong, shoulds or shouldn'ts. It all just *is*. No one could have behaved any differently. The hero does not know why he ran into the burning house any more than the onlookers know why they didn't. It was genetics, upbringing, experiences, and external forces all coming together to create only one answer. It could have been no other way.

Now, knowing what they know *now*, could the man go back in time and *not* run into the house on fire? Could the onlookers go back in time and choose to be heroic, instead? Could the mother go back and choose not to walk down the street for her cigarettes? Could the arsonist go back and not set the house on fire?

No, they can't. *It doesn't exist.*

When I heard it explained like this, it clicked for me. *Everything happens for a reason* because it is all an equation, all cause and effect. And most importantly, it can be no other way. You cannot go back in time and change what happened, because the past does not exist, it only lives in our minds. All we can change is our perception of it now, the meaning we ascribe to it, and the story we choose to tell now.

We are the only living creatures who have the capacity to think in terms of the past. But rather than allowing it to serve as a lesson for the future, and moving on, like a dog with a bone, we gnaw on it relentlessly, thinking about how we can change something that *cannot* be changed, allowing it to *destroy* our present and *create more disruption* in our future.

Ask yourself what patterns, what loops, what lessons keep showing up in your life over and over again? What feelings do you keep feeling? What is your energetic set-point that you keep returning to? What do you continuously recreate for yourself?

Until you can pinpoint these patterns and react differently, shift your perception of them, you will keep serving yourself the same lessons over and over again until you finally master them. This is in regards to any emotion that you find yourself reverting back to time and time again. Do you always feel busy or stressed? Do you always feel inferior or unloved? Do you always feel hurt or pain? Do you always feel frustration or anger?

As Nelson Mandella said upon being released from prison after 27 years, "As I walked out the door toward the gate that would lead to my freedom, I knew If I didn't leave my bitterness and hatred behind, I'd still be in prison." I believe it was also Mandella, although it is often attributed to Buddha and St. Augustine as well, who said, "Holding on to anger is like drinking poison and expecting the other person to die."

Your emotions may seem as though they are based on outside events, but they are within you. You are assigning meaning to events and telling yourself a story, and odds are you are telling yourself the same story over and over again. You must begin telling yourself a new story.

For the suffering to ever end, you must release it. You must let the story end. There is never a need to wonder about rights and wrongs, shoulds and shouldn'ts. The only question you need to ask yourself is whether or not it is useful to think about now. *Is there anything to be done about this now?* If the answer is *no*, you must find a way to move on – to stop thinking about it, to make the decision to stop *creating* more of it.

So now, when I find myself waking in the middle of the night to a thought that immediately fills me with dread, I ask myself, *is there anything to be done about this now?* The answer is typically, *no*. So, I will follow the Rapid Resolution Therapist's advice, and I will say to myself: *There is nothing to be done. It doesn't exist.* I will repeat this phrase over and over again, until the dread leaves me.

This may seem rudimentary. It may seem like it couldn't possibly help. But all your body needs is to be told that what you are thinking about is not actually happening in the now and that there is nothing to be done. Your body will then stop calling you to action, stop giving you the signal that something needs to change. This has saved me countless hours of my life lost in thoughts and emotions that don't serve me, allowing me to put the past in the past and focus on what I can control – the present. I hope it will do the same for you.

Repeat after me: *There is nothing to be done. It does not exist.*

This is how you become one with the Universe – you don't push against it, fighting an impossible fight against what was. Rather, you accept the past for what it is – something that no longer exists – and you leave it where it belongs. You begin looking for pleasure rather than pain, start feeling rather than forcing, and create something new, something better, in the now.

When you want to take away thoughts of the past and the future, ask yourself, *what is wrong in this exact moment?* Typically, the answer to this question is *nothing*. What is wrong is in our mind – it is thoughts or regrets of the past or fears of the future. Even when someone we love has died, our suffering is based only in the imagining of the future moments when they will not be there, based on the past times that they were. In this very moment, the fact that they are not here is not why you suffer. They could just as easily not be here because they are at the grocery store, or better yet, in the next room.

Regretting the past and fearing the future is like asking the Universe for something you don't want. It is putting your conscious attention on an unwanted future outcome. Meanwhile, as the musician Randy Armstrong says, "worrying does not take away tomorrow's troubles, it (only) takes away today's peace."

Live in the now. My anxiety comes mostly during the middle of the night when I wake up from a deep sleep, my mind immediately going to all that was and could be. I look over at my husband snoring lightly next to me, I feel the soft sheets on my skin, I look around at the warm and cozy room that I am in, and I think, *all is well.*

Everything is as it should be. And, in this moment, all is well. And, from this place, I get to decide what I want to create next. I *get to play.* The only question need be, what feels good to do or to have done? This is how I know what to do next.

Joy in the Now

If you were to randomly survey a group of people and ask them what they wanted out of life, what they think would make them happy, I believe you would get some pretty standard answers. People may say things like lots of money, a big house, a nice car, a partner, kids, a successful career, fame, etc.

But if you were to dig into these answers, again, lifting the veil and taking a look at their responses beneath the surface, you would find that all they really want, all they are really striving for, is a *feeling.* They want to *feel* happy. They want to *feel* safe. They want to *feel* loved. They want to *feel* important. They want to *feel* successful. They want to *feel* free.

All any of us are really doing is chasing feelings. We believe that the things listed above – the house, the car, the kids – will bring about these feelings, and that's why we strive for them. But in reality, it is the feelings, *themselves,* that bring about these things. Remember, the Universe, which is *all* energy, is only and always responding to *your* energy. Your energy is quite literally affecting the energy of *everything* around you. When you *feel* the feelings, you align with the vibration of these things, and become a match for them, attracting them to you.

However, if you think these things will bring you happiness when you are not already happy, you will soon come to find that even if you manage to obtain them, they will not likely fulfill your desire for happiness. As the Stoic philosopher, Seneca, said "If what you have seems insufficient to you, then though you possess the world, you will yet be miserable."

This is referred to as the "arrival fallacy" in psychology. People just assume that achieving their goals will bring ultimate happiness. But this is false thinking. True happiness is internal and cannot be brought about by external things.

Alone, these things can not only *not* make you feel how you want to feel, but can often result in making you feel the *opposite*, making you feel lousier than you have ever felt. It can bring about a feeling that all hope is lost and send people into self-destruction mode, because they then think if these things couldn't bring them happiness, then *nothing* will. They begin believing that there is just something intrinsically wrong with them, with no way to fix it.

You must let go of this idea that external things can bring you happiness. Instead, you must look at the here and now and find happiness in this very moment, exactly where you are, regardless of what you do or don't have. You must begin putting a focus back on the simple things in life that bring you joy, that make you feel passionate, that give you purpose. You can still have all of the external things that you desire, but you must understand that if you cannot find happiness within yourself regardless of your external circumstances, then you never will.

I'm here to remind you that the only thing that can bring you happiness is *you*. The only thing that can bring you abundance is the abundance you feel *within*. The only thing that can bring you external love, is the love you have for *yourself*. These internal feelings are what magnetizes the money, the big house, the partner, the success, and even the fame, if that's what is written on your heart.

Remember, God does not play favorites. We are all designed for success, happiness and abundance, as according to *your* internal guidance, no one else's. Every single day you feel nudges, you get intuitive hits, you have a thought that sparks excitement inside of you. Follow these feelings. The nudge you feel toward the tiniest spark of joy has the potential to lead you onto the path of something greater, toward something that lights a fire within you.

When you feel a nudge to stop at that new coffee shop on your way to work, do it. There is no telling what may unfold there. It could be as simple as a delicious latte that brings you a little hit of joy, it could lead to a run-in with the love of your life or a lifelong friend, or the interior design of the shop could inspire you to create something that you'd never dreamed of before.

Your body intuitively knows things that your mind couldn't possibly understand. Listen to what it is telling you to do. And if it makes you fifteen minutes late to work, who really cares? What is that in comparison to a feeling of joy, of love, of creativity, passion, or purpose? Isn't this what life is all about? Isn't that why you are here?

Begin prioritizing what should have always remained a priority – play – and you will experience a life beyond your wildest dreams. The desires you have for your life will begin flowing to you effortlessly, through one magical coincidence, opportunity, synchronicity, serendipity, and miracle after another.

The largest electromagnetic field in the human body is found in the heart. Our hearts actually emit their electromagnetic field *outside* of the body, affecting and influencing the energy fields all around us. This has been measured and proven by science. And guess what creates our electromagnetic field? Guess what affects the energy around us? Our feelings.

Positive emotions generate a harmonious pattern in the heart's rhythm, creating coherence in our entire bodies, putting us in an optimal state for human functioning, which keeps us in perfect health and able to access the full capacity of our creative and critical brains. In addition, these positive emotions emit this coherent state *outside* of our bodies as well, pulling the other energy fields around us into resonance. When we feel good, we emit positivity, we emit love and joy. When we feel good, we make others feel good too.

Our hearts began beating before our brains were ever formed. And Scientists have now found that their electromagnetic energy field is 5000 times greater than the brain's. It is our hearts that send more information to our brain than the other way around. According to Dr. Rollin McCraty, the Research Director of the Heart Math Institute, "Coherence is the state when the heart, mind, and emotions are in energetic alignment and cooperation."

It doesn't start with the thought or the belief or the action. It starts with a *feeling*. And as a result of those feelings, you then know where to focus your thoughts, beliefs, and actions. This is the key to unlocking all that is, all that was, and all that there will ever be. It is the key to unlocking the power of the Universe, the greatness within you, and the key to finding everlasting happiness and success.

Follow your heart, and every feel-good emotion as it comes, and you, too, will create the life of your dreams. Always remember, the life of your dreams is not out there, it is within *you*.

You are your greatest teacher, and once you understand that, you understand everything. There is an infinite intelligence and almighty power that resides within you. Tap into it by letting your feelings be your guide, and then align your every thought, belief, and action to support that which feels good to you.

This is the magic – it is *all* within *you*.

*"If the doors of perception were cleansed, everything
would appear to man as it is, infinite."*

WILLIAM BLAKE

EPILOGUE

"Do not stand at my grave and weep. I am not there. I do not sleep. I am a thousand winds that blow. I am the diamond glints on snow. I am the sunlight on the ripened grain. I am the gentle autumn rain. When you awaken in the morning's hush, I am the swift uplifting rush of quiet birds in circled flight. I am the soft stars that shine at night. Do not stand at my grave and cry; I am not there. I did not die."

MARY ELIZABETH RYE

My husband's father, Karl Richard Littrell, passed away on July 26, 2023, just one day after Kyle's birthday. We believe he held on through that day so as to not cast an eternal shadow over his son's birthday. The love he had for his son was greater than his pain.

We knew Rick was going to die for some time, but knowing someone you love is going to die is not the same as someone you love actually dying. As soon as it happens, you begin thinking about all of the time lost and wondering about all of the precious moments you let slip through your fingers. You review the life of the person you loved, go through old photos, talk about old times, and you think – the only thing that matters, *truly* matters in this life, is love, and joy, and friendship. That's it. Nothing else.

Why does it take losing someone to be reminded of this? And why do we so soon, again, forget this truth? As the weeks and months and years go by, the veil falls back over our eyes, and we find ourselves once again getting caught up in the trivial, the mundane, the schedules, and the responsibilities, and we forget.

We forget how fleeting and fragile and tragic life is. And thus, how *beautiful* life is. Because without loss, we couldn't fully appreciate the beauty and the magic all around us and how special it truly is to love and to be loved.

The brutal reality is that we are all going to die. One day, my husband or I will die, and we will be without each other, just as Kyle's mother is now without his father, the love of her life for nearly 40 years. And I'm sure if you asked her now about those days, and months, and even years that they spent mad at each other over some insignificant thing, or even some important thing, she would tell you that none of that mattered.

She would tell you that it was the years of love, and joy, and friendship, that she remembers now. She would tell you that she would give anything to have him back, despite all of the struggles and the fights, the disappointments and the anger, and that if she could do it all over again, she would – but this time with more appreciation, with more patience, with more joy in her smile, and with more love in her heart.

When my father-in-law passed, Kyle and I were in a really good place. We were physically and emotionally exhausted, as Kyle had been switching off days and nights with his aunt, traveling back and forth to take care of his dad, but the love and affection had returned to our marriage. We had kept our eye on that love and it had grown. I was grateful for that, that we could be there for each other, no chip on our shoulders, just love in our hearts, when he needed it the most.

I think back to the first time that true tragedy struck our lives. We had just graduated college at the time, and were renting a small house together. Kyle had just proposed to me a couple months prior. We were so in love, but far too immature, and still trying to figure out how to trust one another, and how to navigate the big feelings that we had for each other.

Two nights prior, I had gotten mad at him about something stupid. I think he probably deserved it a little bit, in the loose meaning of the term. He had omitted information about an ex-fling hanging out with him and his friends at the bar on his guy's night out.

A picture had been taken of him and posted online that night with a purse sitting on the table next to him. *I thought it was only guys. Who does the purse belong to?* He had told the truth then, but I had already gotten myself worked up and hot, and was ready to fight.

As always, he thought I was nuts and didn't hesitate to tell me so. *He* didn't invite her, after all. She was friends with all of his friends and it was a public bar – It's not like he could have kicked her out!

We weren't speaking, or at least hadn't spoken in over 24 hours. And I was content to let it go on for another 24 hours (or more) until I'd felt like he'd learned his lesson. I wanted him to know that he couldn't get away with not telling me things like that.

Then he had called me at work. I thought about not answering. But something told me to, so I did. His voice was shaky, so low, I could barely make out what he was saying.

"My mom just called. Kody got into an accident at work. I'm on my way to the house to pack a bag and go to the airport. I need to catch a flight back home."

Kyle's younger brother, Kody Dean Littrell, was 26 at the time, and worked as a tree trimmer. He was always talking about the heights to which he had to climb to trim branches, and I remember thinking, *he must have fallen out of a tree*.

I asked Kyle if Kody was going to be okay. "Mom told me I need to get home as soon as possible." Home, for Kyle, was 800 miles away in Massachusetts. No, it did not sound like Kody was going to be okay.

I rushed to the house to meet him and began packing his bag before he got there. When he arrived, he was pale and shaky, his tear-stained face almost unrecognizable. He had talked to his mom again and this time she had told him what she, too, had just learned. Kody had shot himself.

He hadn't gotten into an accident at work, because he had been fired from work several weeks before. He had been leaving the house every morning like he was going to work, but wasn't. No one knew where he had been going or why he hadn't told them the truth, why he'd felt like he'd had to keep it a secret. He had been depressed after his girlfriend had dumped him, too, just recently, but no one knew he was hurting this bad. No one had seen it coming.

Kody was such a good kid, his whole life ahead of him. And instead of confiding in those he loved, instead of asking for help, he'd kept it all buried deep inside, until he imploded. He'd taken his own life to escape the pain. And in doing so, in choosing to give up on his life, he'd torn a hole through the chest of everyone he loved.

I didn't know what to do. I wanted to go with Kyle, I wanted to be there for him. But he told me to stay, to make arrangements for our dog, and to get things in order there. I could come later, there was no reason for me to rush to come right away, and it would just slow him down waiting on me to pack as well.

My anger toward Kyle had obliterated the instant he'd called me with the news, but I couldn't tell if he was still angry with me, and I'd hated myself for it. I wanted to hold him, to cry with him, to get on the plane with him, and to be right there by his side. But he just shrugged me off. And I remember thinking, *how stupid*.

How stupid I had been for fighting with him over nothing, at the same time that he had gotten the worst phone call of his life, when he found out his little brother was in the hospital on life support. And I remember promising myself that I would never do that again. Life was so short and I loved him so much. I would never allow myself to get mad at him like that *ever* again.

I caught a flight the next day to Massachusetts and went to the hospital to be with him. Together, with his parents, we'd made the decision to take Kody off life support far before we were ready, so that his organs could be donated. I held Kyle's hand as his little brother took his last breath. And again, I thought, *I never want to see you hurt like this, I never want to be the source of any of your pain. I will never hurt you again*.

I was there for Kyle when he'd lost his brother and he was there for me when I lost my sister. Together, we had been there for our best friends when they lost their child.

I remember the way my heart ached and lurched out of my chest at the funeral as I watched my dear friends grieve their little boy. The pain in their eyes was so all-consuming, it felt as though it would swallow them whole.

Knox was just a baby, himself, at the time. And I remember thinking, *I'll never complain again about the crying in the middle of the night. I will just thank God that I get to hold him again, that I get to rock him, and feel his warmth, and his beating heart against my chest. I will never, ever forget how lucky I am to be his mother. I will never, ever take motherhood for granted again.*

And now here we were, saying goodbye to Kyle's father, making promises to ourselves once again. Promising to focus more on what really mattered in life, to appreciate more those we loved that were still with us, and to appreciate our own lives more.

Because when the veil lifts, we are faced with the harsh, brutal truth that we are only here for a short time. Here one minute, and gone the next. You are young and full of life and it feels like you will be that way forever. And then, in the blink of eye, you turn around and that youth has slipped through your fingers. And all you can think is, *I should have appreciated it more. I shouldn't have gotten so caught up in things that didn't matter. I should have loved more, had more fun, created more joy. I should have loved myself more and should have done more of what I wanted to do while I had the chance.*

I am reminded of a quote by Marcus Aurelius, an early Stoic philosopher, who said, "You could leave life right now. Let that determine what you do and say and think." Show your appreciation for those you love and for *yourself* more. Don't waste a minute of your life in fear or in doubt. Don't let life pass you by. Go after your dreams. Not because accomplishing them will make you happy, but because it is in the pursuit of those dreams that makes life worth-while. It is the passion and the purpose woven into each and every day that creates a life worth living.

And while you're at it, get everything you want – the money, the clothes, the cars, the home of your dreams. Because, why not? The world *is* your playground, even if just for a short time.

Yes, there will still be faulty equipment, skinned knees and broken arms, kids that make fun of you, kids that don't want to play with you, and sadly, some friends that get sent home too early. But you still get to decide whether or not to keep playing.

You are never too old to play. You are never too old to turn back time. You are never too old to start believing in magic again. In the words of Peter Pan, "Never, ever, grow up."

Always remember that anything is possible. I repeat: *Anything* is possible. And it is *all* within *you*.

EPILOGUE

"To see a world in a grain of sand, and heaven in a wildflower. Hold infinity in the palm of your hand, and eternity in an hour."

WILLIAM BLAKE

In Loving Memory…

KODY DEAN LITTRELL (2002)

Kyle, Knox, Khloe, and Kim

ABOUT THE AUTHOR

Kim Littrell has a Bachelor of Arts in Communication Studies and a Master of Science in Human Resources Leadership. She spent ten years in the retirement plan industry heavily focused on training and development before stepping away to help her husband manage his growing logistics business and pursue her dream of becoming a published author.

As a mother of two, Kim's mission is to change the way the next generation views and interacts with the world and to inspire people of all ages to dream big and create extraordinary lives filled with passion and purpose. She believes that when even just *one* person decides to follow their heart, it changes the world.

Connect with Kim and find more information on her website: https://www.KimLittrellWrites.com